# What people are saying

*"Thank you so much for writing the "Learn Na'vi the Easy Way" activity book. It is my best friend as I start Na'vi and really makes it fun! I just wanted to show appreciation for all the hard work you do . . . Guess you can add me to your list of ppl taught Na'vi. Irayo!"*

*"I did every single exercise in the entire book, some of them twice, and it's easily the single most important reason that I learned the language so quickly."*

*"Your stuff is perfect for that! More, I demand more!"*

*"When I had first started learning the Na'vi language, I eagerly searched for anything that could either speed the process and/or make it easier. When I came across the Na'vi workbook, I was not only amazed at how simple it was to learn the language via this book, but ecstatic at how fun it was too! I would easily recommend this to anyone willing to learn the language in a fun and timely way!"*

*"I've really enjoyed using this book. I think the different activities and learning forms are a helpful and fun way to remember the new vocab."*

*"I'm really a big fan of this. Your book is really where I kicked off my "quest" to learn Na'vi, I printed 3 copies of it so I could work through it more than once, and man, it really did make it a ton easier. When I first came to the forum I couldn't comprehend the whole language, where to start, and what to learn, but then your book came along and it was like the coming of Eywa. I still have all 3 copies with all my answers in them in a binder I keep with all my Na'vi stuff :-)"*

*"It helped me out a lot! Never finished it though . . . But what I did (³⁄₄ of it) did a great job for me!"*

*"I can honestly say that of the little Na'vi I know the main part comes out of the first edition of the Activity Book and my take at translating it. This really is a book that delivers what the title implies: fun lessons that help you learn Na'vi without getting boring. Since Dusty mentioned he was working on a second version I'm anxious to get it into my hands. Let's see how much "Na'vi oe plltxe" afterwards :)"*

# The Easiest Way to Learn Na'vi—*EVER!!*

*Far and away the easiest and
<u>most fun way to learn</u> a new language*

*You are here*

Envisioned, created, designed, and authored by:

## Kaltxì Palulukan!

*(known to the outside world as Dusty White)*

*So what is this book anyway, and why should I read it?*

The purpose of this book is to help you learn Na'vi fast, and as painlessly as possible. Na'vi is a fun, colorful language that is quickly evolving. We have just enough words that *you can learn them all* without too much hard work, but enough to pester your friends with your new language. The problem with learning a new language is knowing where to start, especially without formal instruction. Over the past year we have actively built up various methods of helping each other learn Na'vi. This has all been done at the fan-level, *and on a volunteer basis.* This language has grown organically thanks to the efforts of many talented and dedicated individuals. We have not had the benefit of teachers with classrooms to sit in, no seminars, or instructional DVDs. All we have had is each other yet we wrote books and flash cards, compiled dictionaries, designed software, recorded podcasts and hung out on Facebook. All of this has built up a community of people who know a little Na'vi and share words with each other. **This book is a follow up to *Learn Na'vi the Easy Way!*** and has been written for anyone who wants to learn Na'vi from scratch or help others learn Na'vi quickly and easily. Future volumes, if approved by James Cameron and FOX will expand your vocabulary and syntax.

If you have already read *Learn Na'vi the Easy Way!* you will see some of the previous features repeated in this volume. This is both a revised edition of the previous work and an expansion. Corrections have been made, new words added, and new ways of learning have been implemented. This first volume is intended to be the starting point of a series that will span eight books from absolute beginner to mastery of the language as we know it today. This series is not intended to completely replace other forms of instruction but instead to supplement them, enhancing retention and making the process much more fun.

This first book will focus specifically on building a root vocabulary of useful words that are easy to remember and introducing you to a handful of common phrases. Later volumes will deal with grammar and advanced linguistic terms and concepts. *It is important to have fun doing this and not try to force too much information into your consciousness* at once or you will become frustrated, bored, and angry. Take your time and go at a pace that is comfortable for you but also use the various free learning resources we have listed at the back of the book to help supplement your learning. Find out which iPhone app or podcast *works for you*. Join in on the lessons on TeamSpeak or get over to the forums at learnnavi.org and start asking questions. Use this series to enhance your understanding and retention of words and phrases but look around and you will find that we also have a *"Na'vi Rosetta Stone,"* all kinds of great grammar guides, flash cards, flash card programs, rhyming dictionaries, dictionary software that you can start typing in letters from a Na'vi word and it will intuitively guess what you are looking for and present you with a list of related words.

There are several forums, Facebook groups, Twitter lessons, podcasts, live online lessons and more than a handful of workbooks and worksheets that have been put together to help you learn and it is all free and available 24 hours a day. It's time to start learning and start helping your friends learn as well. At first it will be a little awkward, after all, you are learning a new language. Stay with it. *We are here to help,* and many of us are using different methods to make learning as simple as possible.

My approach is to build your "root vocabulary" quickly and easily, so that when you start studying the more advanced stuff like grammar and all of its subtleties, you will already have a foundation of familiarity with many words. You will be comfortable with the sound of the language, and you will understand how additions to words, like prefixes and suffixes, simply alter words you already know. For example, once you understand the concept of the word "you," *learning the meanings of words like "yours," "you're," and even "y'all" is a breeze.* Root words are affected by alterations, but they retain their "root meaning." Na'vi works a lot like that as you will see. But enough of my yapping. Let's just get right into it. **Ready *srak?***

# How to use this book:

*Print it\*, bind it, read it. (Repeat twice)*

*Best used with a pencil and eraser,*
*but a pen works well too, if you write lightly.*

# How get the most out of this book:

*Start anywhere, really.* The book has been designed to allow you to move progressively forward from page one or to skip around if you get bored. The different exercises and puzzles work together to access different parts of your brain so that you are not always doing the same thing *(memorize and repeat, memorize and repeat . . .)*. as long as you complete all of the exercises at some point you will derive the full value of this material. Please remember to go through this book three separate times to best cement this information so that you will absorb future instruction more easily.

You may already have a working knowledge of some Na'vi, or you may be reading these words wondering what all the excitement is over a movie language that barely has a "thousand known words." If you find this book is "too easy" then you should absolutely use it to teach a friend Na'vi so they can share this "secret language' with you. By the time *Avatar 2* and *A3* come out both of you will be able to shout back at the screen *nì'Na'vi* ("like the Na'vi" or "in Na'vi").

This book focuses primarily on building your vocabulary, so you can understand and actually use basic Na'vi within the next few days. **If you get confused, *don't quit.*** There are dozens of fantastic resources available to you; and they are listed in the back of this book. Try out a few. Get your questions answered, make some new friends, and share what you have learned with others.

Make a commitment to yourself to stay at it; memorize words you like and use them often. Do all of the exercises, activities, and the puzzles in this book. If this book works for you, please write me an email. I am available at *dusty@radioavatar.com.* I want to know that this book is actually out there helping someone.

Okay, irayo *(thank you)* for reading. I hope you will listen to our goofy *Avatar* podcast which can be downloaded from RadioAvatar.com or *radioavatar.podomatic.com.* We yap about all things *Avatar* and occasionally try to learn some Na'vi, which never turns out well, but is fun to listen to our verbal flailings.

— *Dusty White*

---

\* You can have a copy shop like *Kinko's Staples* or *Office Depot* print this book for a few bucks if you don't have immediate access to a black and white printer. It may run you between $5 and $10 per copy. Print three copies! **Two for you, one for a friend!** Remember to do the whole book *again* in a few weeks! **At this time I am asking James Cameron and FOX if we can put up a professionally bound version on Createspace.com.** This would allow you to cover the costs of printing. The end result is that you would get this book in softcover (8"x10" paperback) *professionally printed and bound for just $2.69!* I am making no no money off of this. It is simply a way to *save you a few dollars on printing* and get you a better looking book. At that price you can buy FOUR copies for around ten bucks and get your lazy friends to learn Na'vi too! Or you can do the exercises in this volume four times! **A note on printing:** This book's layout was set to an 8x10 format allowing for a 1/8th" trim. If you print at home or at a copy service *you should print double-sided pages for best effect.*

# Na'vi Flash Cards!

I was going to put these at the end of the book, but given the ever-expanding amount of pages I quickly realized that these cards would become an afterthought or ancillary supplement that may be viewed once or twice but never used. So I put them right up front where they cannot be ignored. **Cut out these flash cards** or take your book to a local copy store and have them copied on cardstock and then use their straight-line cutter to make up a set of flash cards. Simply pull a card for the day and carry it around with you. Glance at it a few times throughout the day and practice your phrase on unsuspecting people (or your cat).

## Na'vi Phrase of the Day

Oel ngati kame
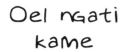

Eywa ngahu!

Ayoeng pivlltxe nìNa'vi ko!

Oel tsa'uti ke tslolam

Ngal pe'uti pìmlltxe?

Tsun oe ngahu pìvängkxo a fì'u oeru prrte' lolu

## Hey you!

<u>Yeah, yeah, you reading this</u>. Go ahead and cut these flash cards out and USE THEM! In fact, get your friends into this. It's free and fun, and when *Avatar 2* comes out you will be able to speak Na'vi just as if you were born on Pandora. Why let *Klingons* have all of the fun?

| | |
|---|---|
| Eywa be with you.<br><br>*(respectful parting)* | I see you.<br><br>*(respectful greeting)* |
| I didn't understand that. | Let's speak Na'vi, okay? |
| It was a pleasure<br>to speak with you. | What did you just say? |

Tsaw lu ngay!

Oel ngaru 'upxareti fpole'.

"Fyape fko syaw ngar?"

"Oeru syaw _____"

Oeru txoa livu

Ngeyä kxetse lu _oeru_!

Ngaru lu fpom srak?

Oeru lu fpom.

" _____ nìNa'vi slu upe?"

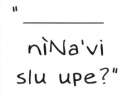

I sent you a message.

That is true!

Forgive me.
*(May I have forgiveness?)*

What's your name?
*(In what way does one call to you?)*

I am _____. / My name is _____.
*(One calls to me _____)*

How are you?
*(Do you have well-being/is well-being to you?)*

I am well.
*(I be well-being)*

You're goin' down!
*(Your tail is mine!)*

I love you.
*(You are beloved to me.)*

How do you say _____
in Na'vi?
*(___ in Na'vi becomes what?)*

# Na'vi Word Flash Cards

Cut out these flash cards or take your book to a local copy store and have them copied on cardstock and then use their straight-line cutter to make up a set of flash cards. You can carry your flash cards and practice them anywhere or tape them up around the house to help you learn words faster.

# So . . .

Did you cut out the flash cards yet? If you need someone to practice your Na'vi with try posting on Craigslist. You may not get any responses but think of all of the people who will see your ad! In fact, why not post an ad in Na'vi? <u>Practice your words</u> and you will have a secret code known only to fans of *Avatar*. Or you can just go on Facebook and friend "Radio Avatar*" and we can all practice together.

\* *Radio Avatar* is a TOTAL fan creation and has <u>absolutely no connection</u> (at this writing) to James Cameron's Avatar™, FOX Studios, Jake Sully, Moat, or Norm Spellman, so it's not like we can get you free tickets or anything. But we might see if we can track down the colonel together as he is such a great villain! *Now let's learn some Na'vi!*

| | |
|---|---|
| **Thanks, or thank you**<br><br><u>Possible responses:</u><br><br>**Kea tìkin** <u>No need</u> (There is no need to thank me / it was nothing)<br><br>**Nìprrte'** <u>Gladly, with pleasure</u> (I did it with pleasure)<br><br>**Oeru meuia** <u>An honor to me</u> (It was an honor to help you) | Kehe! |
| please | **goodbye, or "see ya"**<br><br>*(casual farewell)* |
| ftär<br><br>*(Left)* | **Hello! or Hi!**<br><br>*(casual greeting)* |

| drink

(to _drink_ something) | eat |
|---|---|
| drink

(_something_ to drink) | ask |
| dance | jump |
| error or mistake | choose |

| | |
|---|---|
| evil<br><br>*(noun)* | bad, evil<br><br>*(adjective)* |
| ear | nose |
| eyes<br><br>(pair of eyes) | eye |
| face | mouth |

kllkxem

heyn

fnu

ngeyn

fkxake

hahaw

niä

pom

| | |
|---|---|
| sit | stand |
| tired | quiet<br><br>(be quiet) |
| sleep | itch |
| kiss | grab |

set

tìng mikyun

som

oe

txur

yur

| | |
|---|---|
| now | not |
| listen | next |
| rɢa | tìwew |
| wash | meyp |

**1**

'aw

~~a~~ Partridge in a Pear Tree...

**2**

mune

~~Two~~ Turtle Doves...

**3**

pxey

~~Three~~ French Hens...

**4**

tsìng

~~Four~~ Calling Birds...

**5**

mrr

~~Five~~ Golden Rings...

**6**

pukap

~~Six~~ Geese a Laying...

**7**

kinä

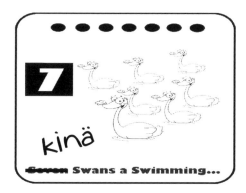

~~Seven~~ Swans a Swimming...

**8**

vol

~~Eight~~ Maids a Milking...

ʼaw, **mune**, pxey, tsìng,
mrr, pukap, kinä, vol

**ʼaw**, mune, pxey, tsìng,
mrr, pukap, kinä, vol

ʼaw, mune, pxey, **tsìng**,
mrr, pukap, kinä, vol

ʼaw, mune, **pxey**, tsìng,
mrr, pukap, kinä, vol

ʼaw, mune, pxey, tsìng,
mrr, **pukap**, kinä, vol

ʼaw, mune, pxey, tsìng,
**mrr**, pukap, kinä, vol

ʼaw, mune, pxey, tsìng,
mrr, pukap, kinä, **vol**

ʼaw, mune, pxey, tsìng,
mrr, pukap, **kinä**, vol

**9** volaw

~~Nine~~ Ladies Dancing...

**10** vomun

~~Ten~~ Lords a Leaping...

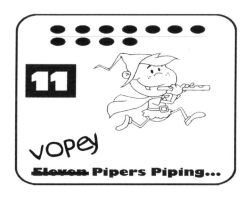

**11** vopey

~~Eleven~~ Pipers Piping...

**12** vosìng

~~Twelve~~ Drummers Drumming...

 pìwopx    taw     pìwopx

aysyulang

tsawke

**MÌN**

eyktan

vomun

*(eight-two)*

volaw

*(eight-one)*

vosìng

*(eight-four)*

vopey

*(eight-three)*

sun

*(From top to bottom)*

cloud      sky      cloud

flowers

leader

*(Not necessarily kawng,*
*although we made this one*
*kawng because it is funny.)*

turn (rotate)

# Na'vi Word Search #1

The purpose of these early word searches is to help you *spot letter patterns* and recognize Na'vi words on sight. This familiarization will make learning and remembering the meanings of new words easier when you start in on the memorization processes. <u>Don't worry about the meanings of these words just yet</u>. Have fun finding them in the puzzles. One thing you will notice immediately are the sets of double letters in the puzzles. Na'vi is an *oral* language. There is no system of notation, no written symbols, no glyphs to indicate letters or sounds. It is only the human need for such artificial devices to teach and communicate that gives us written squiggles we like to call "letters and numbers." As some sounds in Na'vi do not match up to commonly heard words in English we have to create new glyphs to indicate the sounds, but these new marks have to be recognizable to English speakers. The end results are pairs of letters jammed together to indicate a single sound (actual term is "digraph"*). In spoken words this makes no difference, but when writing Na'vi confusion often ensues. To make it easier here <u>we have underlined each letter-pair</u> in the word banks at the bottom of each page.

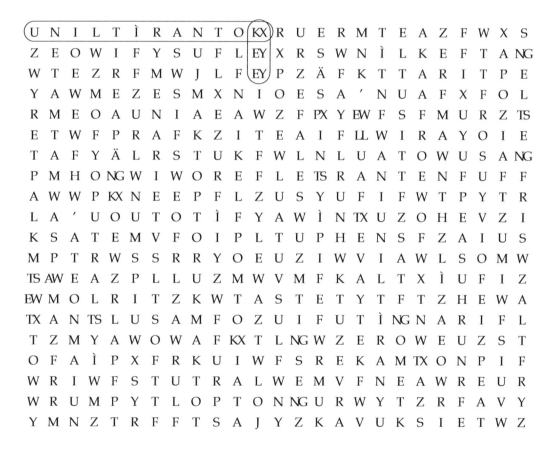

**<u>WORD</u> <u>LIST</u>:** 'UO, ELTU SI, '<u>EW</u><u>LL</u>, FM<u>AW</u>N, FT<u>AW</u>NEMK<u>RR</u>, IR<u>AY</u>O, KAL<u>TX</u>Ì, KAVUK SI, KELFPOMTO<u>KX</u>, <s><u>KX</u><u>EY</u><u>EY</u></s>, LE<u>TS</u>RANTEN, MAKTO, MENARI, MEOAUNIAEA, NÌLKEFTA<u>NG</u>, P<u>AW</u>M, SA'NU, SÄS<u>PX</u>IN<u>TS</u>Y<u>ÌP</u>, S<u>NG</u>EL<u>TS</u>E<u>NG</u>, SREKAM<u>TX</u>ON, TAM TAM, TÌFY<u>AW</u>Ì<u>NTX</u>U, TÌ<u>NG</u> NARI, TÌ<u>NG</u> <u>TS</u>E<u>NG</u>, TIREAPÄ<u>NG</u> <u>KX</u>O, TORUK MAKTO, <u>TS</u>EW<u>TX</u>, <u>TS</u>AW, <u>TX</u>AN<u>TS</u>LUSAM, <s>UNIL<u>TÌ</u>RANTO<u>KX</u></s>, UNIL<u>TÌ</u>RANYU, UTRAL, UTRAL<u>TS</u>Y<u>ÌP</u>

*Technically speaking we can get into the differences between "digraphs" and "dipthongs" but that just makes this a giant fun-vacuum, so we will save the linguistic terminology for a later volume. For now just have fun learning new words.*

# Na'vi Word Search #2

## *(Short words)*

This puzzle contains random common <u>short</u> <u>words</u> you would use in daily conversations. If you know the meaning of a word, great! if not, don't fret over it for a moment. Just use your eyes *(menari)* and brain *(eltu)* together to start spotting the words and letter patterns of the Na'vi language. Then use your eyes *(menari)*, brain *(eltu)*, and hand (<u>*tsyokx*</u>) together to circle the words you find in the puzzle. This may be a bit frustrating at first. That is your brain *(eltu)* getting used to the process. It may seem overtly simple at first. Well, we hope it will. <u>Just</u> <u>have</u> <u>fun!</u>

**WARNING:** This puzzle will start to get mind-numbing after a while. Don't try it all at once.

```
TS  Y   A   L   S   R   A   N   E   Z   T   Ì   Y  AW   N   S   W   V  TS   A   R   I   A   S  TS
M   N   M  LL   T   E   L   A   R   O   O   V   U   T   U   T   E   H   A   K   T   F   K   E   M
U   U   M   U   N   E   S   Y  AY   T   M   S   R   U  NG   Z   M   T   K   E   Ì   W  LL   M   U
K   M   '   R   R   U  TX   E   Z   I   P   O   M   T   I   S   T   I   E   H   F   E   T   P   K
A   E  TS   E  NG   P   E   O   F  TX   A   M   P   A   Y   O   M   F   M   E   N   L   E   U   T
N   L   A   N   L   O   L   N   T   U   H   Z   O   N   A   R   I  TX   R   Z   U   P   Ä   N   U
F   O  TS   U   A   M   I   T   Ì   R   A   N   E   K   A   N   U  EY   H  RR   A   P   I   N   K
Z   N   E   I   H   U   F   U   L   M  PX   H   S   K   I   E   N   F  AW   T   Z  TX   S   W   A
T   U  NG   O   E   M   I   M   A   R   I   A   A   F   T   Ì   L   E   N   U   F   Ä   R   N   M
I   F  KX   U   K   E   E   Y   M   T   U   H   '   T   Ì   R   O   L   U   V   I   R   I   T   E
H   Z   A   T   S   O   Z   Ì   S   Ì   T  AW   N   I   S   A   P   W   O   O   L   E   L   Ì   M
AW  S   N   A   A   N   E   K  LL   P   R   E   W   O   N   O   S   A  TX   O   N   A   M   A   V   U
L   O   Ì   R   T   U   R   V   Z  AW   A   S   K  TS   M   U   K   E   R   I   T   Ì   K  AW  NG
F   K   W   T   Ì   S   O   P   W   M   L   U   W   R   S   E   M   P   U   L   E   A   Z   M   E
Z  AW   Y  AY   M   A   K   E   R   Z   E   F   K  RR   P   E   R   V   K   F   R   A   '   U   I
V   K   N   E   O   W   A   S   P   A   T   T   F   Z   I   A   T   I   R   E   A   F   V   A   R
RR RR   O   M   K   N   W   U   E   M   V   Ì   Y   E   '   K  RR   O   N   T   Ì   K   I   N  AY
T   U   T   E   O   U   Z   F   T   U   E   K   A   K   R   E   L   A   F   R   Ì   P   T   F   O
E   R   S   T   Ì   L   O   R   S  NG   O   A   K   W   Ì   N  TX   U   E   K   V   U   R   V   I
P   F   T   Ì   S   R  AW   R   E   E   Z   N   F   Ä   S   A   '   N   U   F   T   I   A   K   Z
```

**<u>WORD LIST:</u>** FPÌL, FRA'U, FRÌP, FTIA, FTUE, FWEL, HAH<u>AW</u>, HAP<u>XÌ</u>, H<u>AW</u>NU, H<u>RR</u>AP, IRA<u>YO</u>, KAKREL, KAME, KANU, K<u>AW</u>K<u>RR</u>, KEHE, K<u>LL</u>TE, K<u>RR</u>PE, <u>KX</u>ANÌ, <u>KX</u>UKE, LARO, LONU, M<u>LL</u>TE, MUNE, MU<u>NGE</u>, NARI, NEK<u>LL</u>, NUME, OMUM, ONTU, PÄNU, PESU, POE, POM, RENU, R<u>EW</u>ON, RU<u>TX</u>E, SA'NOK, SA'NU, SEMPU, SEMPUL, SKIEN, SRANE, SRU<u>NG</u>, S<u>TX</u>ELI, SYAY, TÌFNU, TÌF<u>TX</u>EY, TÌH<u>AW</u>L, TÌKAN, TÌK<u>AW</u><u>NG</u>, TÌKIN, TÌLAM, TÌLEN, TÌLOR, TÌMOK, TÌP<u>AW</u>M, TÌRAN, TIREA, TÌROL, TÌSOM, TÌSOP, TÌSR<u>AW</u>, TÌSTI, TÌ<u>TX</u>UR, TÌV<u>AW</u>M, TÌY<u>AW</u>N, TOMPA, <u>TS</u>AKEM, <u>TS</u>ARIA, <u>TS</u>A<u>TS</u>ENG, <u>TS</u>E<u>NG</u>PE, <u>TS</u>MUKAN, <u>TS</u>MUKE, <u>TS</u>MUKTU, <u>TS</u>YAL, TUTAN, TUTE, TUTEO, TUVON, <u>TX</u>AMP<u>AY</u>, <u>TX</u>ÄREM, <u>TX</u>EPVI, <u>TX</u>ONAM, UTRAL, VITRA, V<u>RR</u>TEP, VURVI, WEM, WÌN<u>TX</u>U, Y<u>AY</u>MAK, YE'K<u>RR</u>, YOM, YUR, ZAMU<u>NGE</u>, ZEKWÄ, ZEROK, ZÌSÌT

2

# Na'vi Word Search #3

## (Long words)

This puzzle contains random common words you would use in daily conversations. These are long words however, and the point of this particular word search is to train your eyes and frontal lobe to develop pattern-recognition skills in Na'vi "letter arrangement." Keeping in mind that this is only a human approximation of Na'vi sounds, a standardized methodology of letter patterns and word forms will make learning the (audible) Na'vi vocabulary immensely easier. Don't concern yourself with the meanings of these words at present. Just get used to seeing how the letters fit together.

*Quickie alphabet help: When you see an apostrophe in an English word it often shows a contraction, or a "missing letter." (Do not becomes don't.) In Na'vi apostrophes are used to indicate a quick silence, like you would find between words. Think of ' as a consonant; a silent one, just another letter in Na'vi words.*

EXAMPLE: *The word na'vi has 5 (five) distinct sounds: n-a-(silence)-v-i.*

```
L  E  TS U  N  S  L  U  K  M  Y  TS U  H  K  F  U  Y  F  U  Z  K  L  U  S
K  U  A  W  Z  S  U  T  E  U  UNG K  T  Ì  F  M  E  T  O  K  R  E  Y  NG
S  Z  M  K  H  L  Y  R  P  N  Z  AW S  Ì  F  Z  K  P  AW W  E  U  F  K  Ä
Ä  E  S  Y  P  R  K  A  U  TX K  V  L  P  Y  H  I  U  N  A  L  Y  P  H  '
S  P  I  U  A  F  W  L  H  A  O  Ì  U  Ä  K  K  Z  H  E  F  F  K  O  U  I
PX K  Y  Z  M  K  '  TS Y  T  Ì  K  A  NG K  E  M  Y  M  Z  P  U  M  W  Y
I  Y  U  L  R  H  S  Y  K  A  U  P  E  KX I  S  H  K  K  U  O  R  T  K  U
N  W  L  K  E  W  Z  Ì  W  N  Z  K  K  O  Y  F  R  O  RR A  M  S  O  H  K
TS K  F  Y  L  S  K  P  U  U  F  R  A  TS E  NG U  O  E  K  T  L  KX U  Z
Y  Z  S  U  F  U  Z  R  A  Y  S  E  Z  Y  W  O  K  E  U  L  O  Z  R  Y  M
Ì  K  R  W  Y  O  M  T  Ì  NG U  L  K  Ì  Z  I  TS Y  W  R  KX H  K  E  E
P  '  E  K  A  R  K  I  S  M  K  TS A  P  '  A  L  U  T  E  U  L  S  Z  O
W  Z  T  Y  W  W  Y  K  Z  S  E  E  U  H  O  K  E  K  Ì  K  K  H  T  W  A
T  A  R  O  N  Y  U  TS Y  Ì  P  E  O  U  P  Y  S  NG K  Y  W  U  H  A  K  U
K  Z  N  U  P  R  K  K  H  U  N  T  N  K  F  R  H  U  U  L  TX A  R  U  N
H  W  '  L  Z  L  U  S  A  '  N  U  TS Y  Ì  P  U  R  S  F  H  K  S  U  I
I  Y  O  K  P  H  Y  U  K  U  R  Z  W  U  Y  O  W  K  O  Z  L  K  Ì  K  A
K  U  NG W  P  A  M  TS E  O  T  U  S  S  R  E  K  A  M  T  RR V  M  Y  E
U  Z  I  Y  U  Z  K  Y  P  W  U  K  L  U  Z  K  U  H  Y  R  W  O  K  E  A
O  L  O  '  EY K  T  A  N  Z  T  I  R  E  A  P  Ä  NGKX O  I  U  Z  W  K
```

**WORD LIST:** FRA'TSENG, FTAWNEMKRR, KELFPOMTOKX, LEFPOMTOKX, LE'TSRANTEN, LE'TSUNSLU, MEOAUNIAEA, MUNTXATAN, OLO'EYKTAN, PAMRELFYA, PAM'TSEOTU, REL'TSEOTU, SA'NU'TSYÌP, SÄSPXINTSYÌP, SREKAMTRR, SNGÄ'IYU, SRETON'ONG, STARSÌM, TARONYU'TSYÌP, TÌFMETOK, TÌKANGKEM, TÌPÄNG KXO'TSYÌP, TIREAPÄNG KXO, TÌYUSOM, TSAMSIYU, TSAP'ALUTE, 'TS NGAWVÌK, ULTXARUN, UTRAL'TSYÌP, YOMTÌNG

3

# Where do I belong?

This exercise is so easy you will complain that we didn't make it harder. Simply choose words from the "word bank" (at the bottom of the next page) and write it in the group you think it belongs in. The goal here is to get you to be able to spot-categorize words, and get practice writing them. **Ready srak?** Let's *kä* (go) then!

## World

_____     _____

_____     _____

_____     _____

_____     _____

## Body—Mind—Spirit

_____     _____

_____     _____

_____     _____

_____     _____

## Actions and Interactions

_____     _____     _____

_____     _____

_____     _____

_____     _____

# Na'vi Clan Life (specifically)

_____ _____

_____ _____

_____ _____

_____ _____

# Animals & Plant Life

_____ _____

_____ _____

_____ _____

# Word Bank

Choose any of the words here. Ignore any you don't feel like using. You can also use words you know but do not see here on this list.

| KÄ | MIKYUN | AYSMUKÉ | PA'LI | SYAW | TARONYU | NA'RÌNG |
|---|---|---|---|---|---|---|
| go | ear | sisters | dire-horse | call | hunter | forest |
| MOKRI | KELKU | TSAHÌK | FTANG | YAYO | PAWM | TAWTUTE |
| voice | home | spiritual guide | stop | bird | ask | Sky person |
| TRR | YOM | TÄFTXUYU | ATAN | RONSEM | REY | IKRAN |
| day | eat | weaver | light | mind | live | banshee |
| TÌNG | TOMPA | TSAWKE | TAW | UTRAL | HUFWE | PXUN |
| give | rain | sun | sky | tree | wind | arm |
| TXE'LAN | KAME | TSE'A | SYULANG | MUN'I | YE'RÌN | SREW |
| heart | "see" | see* | flower | cut | soon | dance |

*with your eyes*

5

# 2-Letter Words

This exercise is fairly simple. On the left you will find words in English. On the right are spaces to write in the Na'vi word equivalent. <u>Mastering your short words now makes reading sentences in Na'vi later much easier.</u> When words are mutated with *prefixes*, *suffixes*, and *infixes*, knowing the root word pattern will make grammatical variations of a word easier to spot and understand. So, with that in mind, here are some of the known 2-letter Na'vi words. **This is easier than you think.** There is a "word bank" at the bottom of the page. <u>These are all of the 2-letter words you will use in this exercise.</u> Each time you use a word, cross it off. *Start with words you know.* Print extra copies of *this page* and do this exercise once every few days. Please keep in mind that this is not a grammar lesson. Right now we are focusing you on the individual words from English to Na'vi. Grammar comes later, once you have built up a basic vocabulary to work with.

| | English | Na'vi | |
|---|---|---|---|
| 1: | One | AW | "I am number _____. You are not number _____. You are number two." |
| 2: | Thing (object) | U | "What is that, that _____ you brought in? Get that _____ out of my house!" |
| 3: | Things (plural) | AY | "What is have I been up to? Oh, lots of _____. Yeah, many _____ at once." |
| 4: | Lead (not follow) | EY | "_____, follow, or get out of the way! If you don't _____, I will." |
| 5: | Or | F | "Okay, you can have chocolate, _____ vanilla, _____ strawberry, _____ . . ." |
| 6: | So ("in that case . . .") | A | "_____, I guess that means . . ." (or) "_____, what you're saying is . . ." |
| 7: | Next | H | "_____ up we have math, but _____ week the schedule changes." |
| 8: | Go | K | "_____. Just _____. _____ now. I will be fine! Now shoo! _____." |
| 9: | Not | E | "I will _____! _____ today, _____ tomorrow. You now what? _____ ever!" |
| 10: | Zero (0) | K | "Three to _____! Three to _____! We skunked them!" |
| 11: | Face | EY | "Dude! What happened to your _____? Hey! Come look at his _____." |
| 12: | Time | K | "What _____ is it? The _____ is 3:00 here. What _____ is it there?" |
| 13: | Mouth | KX | "Get that out of your _____. Your _____ is not a garbage can." |
| 14: | Lid (cover) | L | "That's the wrong _____. That _____ goes on the spaghetti pot." |
| 15: | Five | M | "_____ bucks? I don't owe you _____ bucks! You owe ME _____ bucks!" |
| 16: | You | A | "_____ and I will eat, then _____ will go home. Take the cat with _____." |
| 17: | Me (or) I | O | "Who *am* _____? _____ am _____! Why would you ask _____ that? |
| 18: | And* | ì | "You _____ I go here. Bob _____ Sue sit there. Jim _____ Mary; over there." |
| 19: | Sky | T | "Did you see the _____ tonight? There is a weird light in the _____." |

> ### WORD BANK
>
> 'AW, 'U, AYU, EYK, FU, HA, HAY, KÄ, KE, KEW,
> KEY, KRR, KXA, LEW, MRR, NGA, OE, SÌ, TAW

\* "And" is represented in Na'vi by two words: <u>Sì</u> is used **when connecting two words** (e.g. "this <u>and</u> <si>that," or "Batman <u>and</u> <si>Robin." <u>Ulte</u> is used **when connecting two clauses.** ("You do this <u>and</u> <ulte>I will do that.")

# 3-Letter Action Words

This is a LOT easier than it looks. <u>Use the word bank</u> as a set of clues.

| | English | Na'vi | |
|---|---|---|---|
| 1: | Cook | ' _ _ | "You _____ dinner. I had to _____ dinner last night." |
| 2: | Answer (respond) | _ EY _ | "_____ them! Or I'll _____ for you." |
| 3: | Chase | _ EW _ | "Tag! You're it! Now _____ me! _____ me!" |
| 4: | Choose | F _ _ | "_____, but _____ wisely." (Avatar was <u>sooo</u> much better than that movie) |
| 5: | Search | _ W _ | "We'll _____ over hear. You guys should _____ over there." |
| 6: | Prepare (get ready) | H _ L | "If you do not _____ yourself for success you _____ for failure." |
| 7: | Sit | _ _ N | "_____ down, _____ down. Make yourself at home!" |
| 8: | Leave (depart) | H _ _ | "We should _____ now. If we _____ now we can make it." |
| 9: | Teach | _ A _ | "If you _____ me Spanish I will _____ you Na'vi." |
| 10: | Repeat | L _ _ | "Again! Do it again! _____! _____! THAT is how you learn." |
| 11: | Drink | _ Ä _ | "Eat, _____, and be merry! And then _____ some more!" |
| 12: | Create | NG _ _ | "I want you to _____ something for me. _____ me a masterpiece!" |
| 13: | Grab | _ _ Ä | "Don't just _____ things. It is not polite to _____ at things!" |
| 14: | Ask | _ AW _ | "Go ahead and _____. _____ me anything! The answer is NO!" |
| 15: | Tell | _ _ NG | "_____ me dear Colonel. What exactly <u>did</u> you _____ the Na'vi?" |
| 16: | Kiss | P _ _ | "Bah! _____ her already! How hard is it to _____ a pretty girl?" |
| 17: | Move | _ _ KX | "Don't _____ a muscle. If you _____ even one inch . . ." |
| 18: | Sing | _ _ L | "Aw c'mon, _____ us a song. Your mother used to _____ for us." |
| 19: | Discover (find) | _ U _ | "_____ what the RDA is up to. _____ that and you get a raise." |
| 20: | Use | _ A _ | "Oh, never _____ a bullet when a blade will do! _____ this one." |
| 21: | Jump | S _ _ | "You will _____ when I say _____! You will _____ high and fast." |
| 22: | Dance | _ R _ | "Tomorrow we fight. TONIGHT we _____! We _____ for life!" |
| 23: | Give | _ Ì _ | "_____ us a coin then? One little coin is a small thing to _____." |
| 24: | Squirt | _ _ ' | "Ugh! Don't _____ me with that! _____ me again and I swear . . ." |
| 25: | Allow | T _ _ | "I will _____ you this one time, but I will never _____ it again!" |
| 26: | Leave (abandon) | _ _ _ | "We need to _____ this place. It is now RDA territory." |
| 27: | Draw | W _ _ | "_____ it like this. Watch me _____ it, then you _____ it." |
| 28: | Eat | _ _ M | "You should _____ now while you can. _____ or wait until night." |
| 29: | Wash | _ U _ | "Be sure to _____ before you (yom). _____ your hands AND face." |
| 30: | Scream | Z _ _ | "Don't _____ at me. In fact, don't _____ at all. It's annoying." |

---

## WORD BANK

'EM, 'EY<u>NG</u>, F<u>EWI</u>, FT<u>XEY</u>, FW<u>EW</u>, H<u>AWL</u>, H<u>EY</u>N, HUM, KAR, L<u>EY</u>N, NÄK, <u>NG</u>OP, NIÄ, P<u>AWM</u>, P<u>E</u>NG, POM, RI<u>KX</u>, ROL, RUN, SAR, SPÄ, SR<u>EW</u>, TÌ<u>NG</u>, <u>TS</u>Ä', TU<u>NG</u>, T<u>XÌNG</u>, W<u>EY</u>N, YOM, YUR, Z<u>AW</u><u>NG</u>

# Practice your words! (1)

In order to remember the words you have just learned it is important to use them in actual context. Please remember that we are not concerned with the niceties (*or <u>complexities</u>*) of grammar just yet. We are just using simple word substitution of the short words you are working on right now so that we can add them to your list of known words, your Na'vi vocabulary. This is an open-book test and you should flip back over the past few pages when you find yourself needing to be reminded of a particular word. Okay, **ready srak?**

\_\_\_\_\_ _____ \_\_\_\_\_ should learn is to \_\_\_\_\_. \_\_\_\_ \_\_\_\_\_ and \_\_\_\_\_ will \_\_\_\_\_ \_\_\_\_\_ \_\_\_\_\_ \_\_\_\_\_ to
(One)  (thing)  (you)                   (cook)  (Ask)  (me)    (I)      (teach)  (you) (five)  (things)

_____. If \_\_\_\_\_ \_\_\_\_\_ \_\_\_\_\_ \_\_\_\_\_ \_\_\_\_ will _____ up and _____ \_\_\_\_\_ with water until \_\_\_\_\_
(create)      (you)  (sing)  (and)  (dance)  (I)    (jump)      (squirt) (you)                (you)

\_\_\_\_\_ \_\_\_\_\_ _____ \_\_\_\_\_ _____ \_\_\_\_ away.
(sit)  (and)  (scream)  (or)  (chase)  (me)

\_\_\_ will \_\_\_\_\_ \_\_\_\_\_ to the chief. Look at his \_\_\_\_\_ and \_\_\_\_\_ your \_\_\_\_\_ to _____ him if \_\_\_\_ can
(I)    (lead)  (you)                      (face)     (use)     (mouth)   (ask)         (you)

\_\_\_\_\_ his daughter. _____ should _____ the question and \_\_\_\_\_ his arm. Make him _____ to \_\_\_\_ with
(kiss)            (You)        (repeat)               (grab)           (choose)  (go)

\_\_\_\_\_ \_\_\_\_ \_\_\_\_. _____ to _____ quickly though.
(you)  (or)  (not)  (Prepare)    (leave)

## How easy is this?

\_\_\_\_\_ should \_\_\_\_\_ \_\_\_\_\_ \_\_\_\_\_ tell.
(You)      (not)  (kiss)  (and)

It's \_\_\_ \_\_\_\_ to \_\_\_\_\_ yet. \_\_\_\_ should \_\_\_\_\_ first. It is \_\_\_\_ to \_\_\_\_\_ \_\_\_ how to \_\_\_\_\_ \_\_\_\_ \_\_\_\_\_.
(not) (time)    (eat)    (You)    (wash)      (time)  (teach) (me)     (sing)  (and)  (dance)

If \_\_\_\_ _____at \_\_\_ \_\_\_ will _____.
(you) (jump)  (me) (I)    (scream)

\_\_\_\_\_ _____ \_\_\_ _____for. \_\_\_\_\_ should _____ a \_\_\_\_\_ on that \_\_\_\_ in the \_\_\_\_. It looks like a _____.
(Five) (things)  (I)  (search)    (You)    (draw)  (mouth)    (face)   (sky)             (lid)

## Okay, now it's your turn!
(Simply write a few sentences using as many new Na'vi words you just learned.)

_____

_____

_____

*\* Please note that here the word "and" (si) is used when connecting <u>two words</u>. We have not learned the OTHER word for "and" yet, which is <u>ulte</u>. Ulte is used when connecting two clauses (which we will find out more on later).*

# 3-Letter Adjectives

| | English | Na'vi | |
|---|---|---|---|
| 1: | Exciting | _ _ ' | "That party was so _____! More_____ than watching TV." |
| 2: | Blue* | _ A _ | "The sky is _____ but the sea is _____ too. So are air and water _____?" |
| 3: | Right (correct) | _ _ R | "You are _____ sir. For once today, you are indeed _____." |
| 4: | Mighty | _ K _ | "You are not _____! Toruk Makto is _____! You are a ngawng!" |
| 5: | Previous | H _ _ | "That _____ comment was unintentional." |
| 6: | Bit (Small amount) | ' _ _ | "There's a _____ of it over here. Not much, just a _____." |
| 7: | Few | _ _ L | "I only have a _____ coins left. She may have a _____ as well." |
| 8: | Bad (evil) | _ AW _ | "That Colonel's a _____ man! You stay away from him! He's _____!" |
| 9: | High | KX _ | "_____ up in the tree you find push fruit. You, climb _____ now." |
| 10: | Calm | M _ _ | "_____! Be _____! I chased those RDA scum back to their base." |
| 11: | Weak | _ _ P | "Bah! Sawtute vrrtep are _____. _____ minded, _____ of will too." |
| 12: | New | _ I _ | "YOU need a _____ ikran! Buy a _____ ikran at Craaaazy Carl's!" |
| 13: | Tired | _ _ N | "I am so _____ of this. I am so _____ I might just take a nap." |
| 14: | Worthy | PX _ | "You're not _____ to buy ikran from Crazy Carl! But I am _____." |
| 15: | Yellow | R _ _ | "I have a _____ ikran, a matching _____ saddle, and a _____ . . ." |
| 16: | Hot | S _ | "Don't touch that. It's _____. Use a glove when holding _____ things." |
| 17: | Best | _ W _ | "Is that the _____ deal you can give me Carl? I want the very _____!" |
| 18: | Full | T _ _ | "It is hard to fill a cup that is already _____. Is yours _____?" |
| 19: | White | _ _ R | "I don't want a yellow ikran. I want a _____ one! _____ like snow!" |
| 20: | Low | Ì _ | "You have to duck _____ here. Very _____ or you hit your head." |
| 21: | Last | O _ | "This is the _____ time; you hear me? The _____ time!" |
| 22: | Dirty | _ _ TX | "Ugh! You are _____! Your clothes are _____, Your hair . . ." |
| 23: | Brave | _ _ EW | "He . . . is _____. His son, not so _____." |
| 24: | Closed (shut) | TS _ | "Case _____. I _____ it and I refuse to reopen it, just for you." |
| 25: | Awake | TX _ | "Okay! I'm _____! I'm _____! Now where's the coffee?" |
| 26: | Strong | _ U _ | "You are not very _____. You must be _____ to be tsamsiyu." |
| 27: | Dry | U _ _ | "Here's a towel. _____ yourself off. Then _____ the towel there." |
| 28: | Fast | W _ _ | "Wow, that went by _____. So _____ I never got to take that nap." |
| 29: | Loud | _ _ K | "_____ music, _____ voices, _____ people. This party is too _____!" |

---

## WORD BANK

'IT, 'O', EAN, EY AWR, FKEW, HAM, HOL, KAW NG, KX AYL, MAW EY,
MEYP, MIP, NG EYN, PXAN, RIM, SOM, SWEY, TEYA, TEYR, TÌM, TOR,
TS EW TX, TSTEW, TSTU, TXEN, TXUR, UKXO, WIN, WOK

*Technically, "ean" means both blue AND green. But for the moment let's just call it blue.

# Useful 3-Letter Words

*Note:* You may notice some words from previous lists. This is intentional and designed to reinforce your working vocabulary.

| | English | Na'vi | |
|---|---|---|---|
| 1: | Plant | ⊔ | *"I bought a _____ from the nursery. It's a small _____ but I like it."* |
| 2: | Answer *(respond)* | ' | *"_____ me. And when you do _____ do so politely."* |
| 3: | Busy *(occupied)* | ì | *"The boss is _____ now. Come back when he is not _____."* |
| 4: | Tiny bit | T | *"This _____ is all I get? You give me only a _____?"* |
| 5: | Something | ⊔ | *"Let me tell you _____. _____ is better than nothing at all."* |
| 6: | Instance | A | *"Well, one _____ when I went crazy; another _____ I forgot . . ."* |
| 7: | Succeed | Ä | *"_____ or fail. What do I care? If you _____ I also _____."* |
| 8: | Throat | F | *"She says her _____ is sore. Her _____ is raw from shouting."* |
| 9: | Quiet | N | *"_____ down now. All you you just _____ so I can think . . ."* |
| 10: | Tongue | TX | *"Bite your _____. Keep silent or you may have no _____ at all."* |
| 11: | Search *(look for)* | W | *"_____ over there. I will _____ over here and see if I find it."* |
| 12: | Teach | K | *"I _____ you Na'vi, then you _____ your friends Na'vi."* |
| 13: | Bad *(evil)* | AN | *"This is _____. Really _____. How can we fix this mess?"* |
| 14: | Deed *(action)* | M | *"This _____ you do cannot be undone. Will you do this _____?"* |
| 15: | Spin | ì | *"All this learning makes my head _____. _____ like a top."* |
| 16: | Need | N | *"I _____ a Pop-Tart. I want coffee but I ** _____ ** a Pop-Tart!"* |
| 17: | Also *(too)* | P | *"Do you want a Pop-Tart _____? You _____? You got it!"* |
| 18: | Middle | KX | *"Cut that Pop-Tart in the _____. That's not the _____!"* |
| 19: | Maybe | AN | *"_____ you didn't hear me, or _____ you wanted all of it."* |
| 20: | High | AY | *"How _____? You jump this _____ and you can have one too."* |
| 21: | Mistake | EY | *"You made a _____ taking my Pop-Tart. A big _____."* |
| 22: | Appear *(seem)* | A | *"It would _____ that we are lost. Does that _____ true to you?"* |
| 23: | Obey *(heed)* | k | *"If I _____ your advice I cannot _____ my orders from the boss."* |
| 24: | Happen *(occur)* | E | *"When did this _____? Did it _____ here? How did it _____?"* |
| 25: | Repeat | EY | *"_____! Do it right this time and then _____ and _____."* |
| 26: | Approach | L | *"_____ the yerik slowly. _____ quietly or you scare it away."* |
| 27: | Reason *(excuse)* | ⊔ N | *"_____? I need no _____ to see the chief!"* |
| 28: | Calm | M | *"Don't you tell me to be _____. I am _____. You need to be _____."* |
| 29: | Weak | M P | *"You are _____ minded. _____ people get pushed around."* |

---

## WORD BANK

'EWLL, 'EYNG, 'ÌN, 'IT, 'UO, ALO, FLÄ, FL<u>EW</u>, FNU, F<u>TX</u>Ì, FW<u>EW</u>, KAR, K<u>AWNG</u>, KEM, KÌM, KIN, KOP, <u>KX</u>AM, <u>KX</u>AWM, <u>KX</u>AYL, <u>KX</u>EY<u>EY</u>, LAM, LEK, LEN, L<u>EY</u>N, LOK, LUN, M<u>AWEY</u>, M<u>EY</u>P

# Practice your words! (2)

First, _____ your milk and _____ something, _____. _____ _____ should _____ a _____ _____ _____
     (drink)              (eat)              (fast)  (Next) (you)        (choose)   (yellow) (or) (white)

_____to _____, _____ a _____ _____. Here's a _____ to _____. Be careful. It is _____. _____ and _____
(thing)  (cook)  (not)  (blue) (thing)          (lid)    (use)                  (hot)   (Wash)      (dry)

it after _____ have made sure it is _____. _____ _____ do _____ _____ in your _____. While _____ are cooking,
          (you)                    (shut) (Dirty) (things)   (not) (go)        (mouth)        (you)

be sure to _____, _____, _____, and _____ about, but do _____ _____ for more than _____ minutes. It is _____
            (move)  (jump)  (sing)      (dance)           (not)  (sit)              (five)            (time)

_____ got some exercise. _____, _____ yourself, for only _____ _____ _____ warriors become _____
(you)                     (Also)  (prepare)                (worthy) (and)  (brave)               (strong)

_____ _____. _____ warriors _____ only on _____ rocks.
(and) (mighty) (Weak)        (sit)         (low)


If _____ get _____ _____ a _____ _____ and _____ it a _____ times. _____ a cup to _____ from until
   (you)     (tired) (grab)   (new) (plant)    (spin)    (few)         (Use)         (drink)

_____ are _____. Do _____ be _____. _____ _____ so that others hear _____ and stay _____ as well.
(you)     (awake)    (not)   (quiet) (Sing) (loud)                   (you)          (awake)

_____ have no _____ _____ to _____ _____ _____. _____ _____ when _____ _____ _____ perfectly,
(You)         (reason) (not)   (teach) (and) (lead) (You) (succeed)      (you) (repeat) (action)

_____ when _____ _____ _____ out of habit.
(not)       (you) (repeat) (action)

## Okay, now it's your turn!
(Maybe you can come up with better sentences. Use 2- and 3-letter words from the previous exercises.)

# Commonly Used 4-Letter Words

| | | | |
|---|---|---|---|
| 1: | Once *(occurence)* | ___ Aw ___ ___ | "_____ upon a time. It's always _____ upon a time . . ." |
| 2: | First | ___ ___ V E | "I came in _____. Being _____ gives me the best seat." |
| 3: | Second | ___ U V ___ | "You came in _____. _____ is not first. That means I win." |
| 4: | Third | PX ___ ___ ___ | "_____? _____ is not even an option. First is an option." |
| 5: | Fourth | ___ ì ___ ___ | "That was the _____ slice of pie I had today. The _____!" |
| 6: | Fifth | ___ RR ___ ___ | "He's _____ in line. If you want to be _____, get in front of him" |
| 7: | Sixth | P ___ ___ ___ | "_____ ain't so bad. _____ out of 100 means you are at the top." |
| 8: | Seventh | ___ ì ___ ___ | "The _____ number in Na'vi is next to last in a set." |
| 9: | Feel *(sense)* | ___ E ___ ___ | "I _____ a change coming. Can you _____ it , really _____ it?" |
| 10: | Young | ___ Ew ___ | "You are _____ for a taronyu; far too _____ to be a tsamsiyu." |
| 11: | Light *("not dark")* | ___ T ___ N | "Let some _____ in this place!" You need _____ to read by." |
| 12: | Brain | ___ ___ T U | "Think with your _____, not your heart next time. Your _____." |
| 13: | Smell | F ___ H ___ | "Can you _____ that? I can _____ something strange." |
| 14: | Today | F ___ ___ RR | "If _____ was tomorrow yesterday than _____ is yesterday tomorrow." |
| 15: | Send | ___ P E ___ | "_____ me an invitation. I will _____ you a reply when I can." |
| 16: | Think | ___ ___ ì ___ | "If you _____ I am in charge then I _____ you are confused." |
| 17: | Bite | ___ R ì ___ | "Go on, take a _____. Just a little _____. It won't kill you." |
| 18: | Guest *(visitor)* | F ___ T ___ | "You are our _____ here. Our honored _____ in fact." |
| 19: | Left *(opposite of "right")* | ___ ___ Ä ___ | "Turn _____ here. _____, _____! Oh, you missed it." |
| 20: | Study | F T ___ ___ | "_____ your lessons well. careful _____ makes you wise." |

*Now try making a few simple sentences using the words above*

---

### WORD BANK

'AWLO, 'AWVE, MUVE, PXEYVE, TSÌVE, MRRVE, PUVE, KIVE, 'EFU, 'EWAN,
ATAN, ELTU, FAHEW, FÌTRR, FPE', FPÌL, FRÌP, FRRTU, FTÄR, FTIA

12

# Other 4-Letter Words You Should Know

1: Easy     F _ T _     *"This is _____ once you get the hang of it. Very _____."*

2: Broken     _ W E _     *"Why is this _____? It was not _____ when I left this morning."*

3: Sleep     H _ H _     *"_____ eludes me tonight. I may have to _____ tomorrow."*

4: Part *(part of something)*     H A _ _     *"My dog is _____ Nordic wolf and _____ poodle. I call it a . . . "*

5: Finished *(done)*     _ A S _     *"I'm _____. I am going to eat. Join me when you are _____."*

6: Tiny, little, small     _ Ì _ '     *"That kitten is so _____. I think I will call it '_____ bit of fluff'."*

7: Second *(unit of time)*     H _ K _     *"Now hold on just a _____. Give me a _____ to sort this out."*

8: Intricate     _ _ N O     *"Na'vi philosophy is an _____ weave. _____ and close-knit."*

9: Danger     _ RR _ _     *"_____! _____ Will Robinson! You are in great _____!"*

10: Thanks     _ R AY _     *"_____ for helping with dinner. Sarah says _____ as well."*

11: See *(understand, know)*     K _ _ E     *"Others see you, but I _____ you. I _____ you completely."*

12: Smart *(intelligent)*     _ _ N U     *"You are pretty _____ for a sawtute. Yes, _____. I will watch you."*

13: Rhythm     _ A _ T     *"She danced with such a _____ I was entranced."*

14: Never     _ AW _ RR     *"You will _____ enter the temple. Do you hear me? _____!"*

15: Nothing     _ E _ '     *"You lose. you get _____. There is _____ for you here. Now go."*

16: No!     K _ H _     *"_____, _____, a thousand times _____. Now excuse me please."*

17: Incorrect     _ EY AW _     *"You sir, are _____! yes, an _____ answer gets you nothing."*

18: Bottom *(opposite of top)*     _ LL P _     *"I was at the _____ of the dogpile. Being on the _____ sucks."*

19: Ground *(dirt, soil, land)*     _ LL _ E     *"You stand on sacred _____. This _____ is not your place to be."*

20: When     _ RR P _     *"_____ will you start helping out around here? _____ I am dead?"*

## *Now try making a few simple sentences using the words above*

_____

_____

_____

_____

---

### WORD BANK

FTUE, FWEL, HAH<u>AW</u>, HA<u>PX</u>Ì, HAS<u>EY</u>, HÌ'I, HÌK<u>RR</u>, HÌNO, H<u>RR</u>AP, IR<u>AY</u>O,

KAME, KANU, KATO, K<u>AWKRR</u>, KE'U, KEHE, K<u>EY AW</u>R, K<u>LL</u>PA, K<u>LL</u>TE, K<u>RR</u>PE

# More 4-Letter Words You Should Know

1: Forbidden    KX _ _ _      *"These demons are _____ here."*

2: Safe *(protected)*    _ _ K E      *We are _____ here. _____ from harm, _____ from the night."*

3: Enemy    _ _ T U      *"I am not your _____. The colonel is the _____."*

4: Clean *("dirt-free")*    L _ _ O      *How do you get your dishes so _____ ? I want _____ dishes!"*

5: Black    _ AY O _      *"Not everything is _____ & white. Chess pieces are _____ & white."*

6: Daily    L _ T _      *"if you study Na'vi _____ you will speak it fluently in 2-3 months."*

7: Word    _ Ì _ '      *"The Na'vi _____ for hello is kaltxì. The _____ for goodbye . . ."*

8: Let go *(release)*    L _ N _      *"_____ of me. _____ me now. Do you know who I am?"*

9: After *(afterwards)*    _ AW _ RR      *"'Happily ever _____?' There will be nothing left _____ this."*

10: Twice    M E _ _      *"I think I asked _____ now. Yes, _____ it was. But I'm still waiting."*

11: Inside    M Ì _ _      *"_____ or out please. But stay _____ or stay outside."*

12: Agree    _ _ T E      *"Oh I _____. I _____. You are right sire; you are always right."*

13: Take, or bring    _ _ NG _      *"_____ that here please. Okay, now _____ it to Andrew."*

14: Eye    N _ _ I      *"I spy with my brown _____." (Kinda kills the rhyme, doesn't it?)*

15: Up    N _ F _      *" '_____, _____, and away', the man in the blue tights used to say."*

16: Down    N _ K _      *"_____? You can't get _____ there from here. Take the stairs."*

17: Next    _ Ì _ AY      *"Okay, I am _____. Then you, and you are _____ after that."*

18: Truly    _ Ì NG _      *"_____, you have a dizzying intellect." (Princess Bride quote)*

19: Learn    N _ M _      *"Once you _____ Na'vi, you can help your friends _____ Na'vi."*

20: Hungry    _ _ KX _      *"I'm _____! Moooommmmmm! I'm _____! Feed me!"*

*Now try making a few simple sentences using the words above*

_____

_____

_____

_____

_____

---

## WORD BANK

KXANÌ, KXUKE, KXUTU, LARO, LAYON, LETRR, LÌ'U, LONU, MAWKRR, MELO, MÌFA, MLLTE, MUNGE, NARI, NEFÄ, NEKLL, NÌHAY, NÌNGAY, NONG, NUME, OHAKX

14

# Even More 4-Letter Words You Should Know

1: Clan     O \_\_\_\_     *"These are not just my friends. This is my _____; my tribe."*

2: Know     \_\_ M \_\_ M     *"I _____, I _____, you are more popular than everyone . . ."*

3: Nose     \_\_ N T \_\_     *"Bee on my _____! Bee on my _____! Get it off, quick!"*

4: Side     \_\_ \_\_ ' O     *"Paint this _____ of the fence then paint that _____."*

5: Promise     \_\_ Ä \_\_ U     *"_____ me this: You will never go back on a _____ to me."*

6: When     \_\_ E H \_\_     *"_____ will we get there? _____ will we be at home?"*

7: Who     \_\_ E S \_\_     *"_____ is that? _____ is there?"*

8: Open     \_\_ I \_\_ K     *"I can't _____ the door; may hands are full. Can you _____ it?"*

9: Speak     \_\_ LL TX \_\_     *"_____ your mind here. Go ahead; _____. Say anything you like."*

10: Head     R \_\_ \_\_ '     *"This melon is your \_\_\_\_\_. Well it's not really your \_\_\_\_. It's a . . ."*

11: Pattern     \_\_ \_\_ N U     *"This \_\_\_\_\_ of behavior is different from the \_\_\_\_ he showed before."*

12: Morning     \_\_ EW \_\_ N     *"Good _____! Good _____ everyone. Let's start the day right."*

13: Please     R \_\_ TX \_\_     *"_____ daddy! _____, _____, _____, _____, buy me a pony!"*

14: Lip     S \_\_ EY \_\_     *"I cut my _____. See? It got me right here on my _____."*

15: Idiot *(moron)*     S \_\_ \_\_ \_\_     *"What a _____. Not just a _____ but a tawtute _____!"*

16: Chance *(opportunity)*     \_\_ KX \_\_ M     *"Go ahead. Take a _____! You may not get a _____ like this again."*

17: Sick     S \_\_ PX \_\_     *"I'm not really _____. I am just calling in _____ to work."*

18: Help *(assistance)*     \_\_ R \_\_ NG     *"You need _____ with Na'vi. I will _____ you – for a price."*

19: Hear     \_\_ \_\_ AW M     *"'I _____ you,' is not the same as 'I see you.' _____, see; different."*

20: Almost     S \_\_ \_\_ U \_\_     *"_____ is not good enough. _____ is failure. It is incomplete."*

## *Now try making a few simple sentences using the words above*

_____

_____

_____

_____

---

### WORD BANK

OLO', OMUM, ONTU, PA'O, PÄNU, PEH**RR**, PESU, PIAK, P**LL**TXE, RE'O, RENU,
R**E**WON, RU**TX**E, S**E**YRI, SKX**AW**NG, SKXOM, SP**X**IN, SRU**NG**, ST**AW**M, STUM

# 5-Letter Verbs

1: Touch     ʼ    M      "Don't _____ that! It is too hot to _____ right now."

2: Move      Ä     P    "If you won't _____ dad's car, then will you _____ mom's?"

3: Stay     Ì    Aɴ    "_____. Don't go yet. You have time, so _____ with me."

4: Itch     KX      "Arrrgh! I've got this _____ in my foot that won't go away!?"

5: Stand     LL KX      "_____, sit, kneel. _____, sit kneel; all day long. And what for?"

6: Ride    M    K      "Okay, let's _____! You _____ with me."

7: Cut           "Never _____ towards yourself. You will _____ yourself!"

8: Arrive       ʼ    I    "We _____ JFK at 7, but we won't _____ at the party until 10."

9: Decide   P      ʼ      "Until you _____ on a pet we will be here all day."

10: Wish      Nɢ     L   "Make a _____! Blow out the candles and make a _____!"

11: Destroy   S   K      "I will _____ you. Then I will be grand-master of HALO!"

12: Produce   S   L     U   "Until you _____ results you are on probation."

13: Anger *(enrage)*   S   T      "Oh, don't _____ the bunny. If you _____ him he may attack."

14: Walk      R   A   N   "First you _____ over here. Then _____ here a bit and . . . "

15: Throw   TS      ʼ    "_____ me the ball! _____ me the ball!"

16: Rest    TS      KX   "You should _____ while you can. _____ now."

17: Fly      W   Aɴ    "Can you _____? I thought all wizards could _____."

18: Lean      U     O   N   "You can _____ on me. _____ on me anytime you need."

19: Show     Ì    TX    "_____ me. _____ me where your ikran is right now!"

20: Remember       K   "_____; the best way to _____ a thing is to <u>feel</u> it."

*Now try making a few simple sentences using the words above*

_____

_____

_____

_____

---

**WORD BANK**

ʼAMPI, ʼÄRÌP, ʼÌ<u>AW</u>N, F<u>KX</u>AKE, K<u>LL</u> <u>KX</u>EM, MUNʼI, PEʼUN, RA<u>NG</u>AL, SKAʼA,

SL<u>EY</u>KU, ST<u>EY</u>KI, TÌRAN, <u>TS</u>REʼI, <u>TS</u>URO<u>KX</u>, <u>TS</u>W<u>AY</u>ON, TUVON, WÌN<u>TX</u>U, ZEROK

# Fun 5-Letter Adjectives

1: Worst — ' _ _ ' _ — *"Ugh! This is the _____ day of my life! The absolute _____!"*

2: Cowardly — F _ N _ _ — *"Stop being so _____. _____ men never get to be chief."*

3: Funny *(strange)* — Ħ _ _ ì _ — *"He is a _____ one. He has _____ eyes. All humans do."*

4: Sweet *(taste)* — _ A _ L I — *This pie is _____. It may even be a bit too _____ for me."*

5: Unhappy *(upset)* — _ _ F TX O — *"Why are you _____? You weren't _____ earlier today."*

6: Slow — K _ _ _ NG — *"Your ikran is too _____. Why did you get a _____ one?"*

7: Brown — _ LL _ AN — *"I swear I just saw a _____ nantang. A _____ one!"*

8: Heavy — _ U _ U _ — *"How _____ is that? Is that too _____ for you to carry?"*

9: Excessive — L _ Ħ _ _ — *"Your chatter is _____. _____ talk will not be tolerated."*

10: Useful — _ _ S A R — *"Make yourself _____. Grab a broom. Ian is _____. See?"*

11: Sufficient — L _ _ A M — *"That will be _____ to hold you. Will that be _____?"*

12: Married *(mated)* — _ U _ TX _ — *He _____ her sister and she _____ his brother."*

13: Difficult *(hard)* — _ _ Z _ _ — *"This is too _____. I don't like _____ things. I like easy things!"*

14: Fresh — PX _ S U _ — *That donut doesn't look too _____. Better grab a _____ one."*

15: Handsome — _ AY _ _ P — *"I am _____, strong, and modest! Did I mention I am _____?"*

16: Pretty* — S _ V _ _ — *"You look _____ in that dress. Very _____ indeed."*

17: Right *(opposite of left)* — _ K _ E N — *"Turn _____ here. Turn _____, quick! No, your other _____!"*

18: Unfamiliar *(strange)* — _ TX _ NG — *We are in _____ territory here. This is all _____ to me."*

19: Bitter *(taste)* — _ _ Ä _ Ä — *"Eww! Bleh! That is _____! Here, try it. It's _____, right?"*

20: Foolish *(ignorant)* — Y AY _ _ K — *"You are _____, like a child. Brave, but _____; and stupid!"*

*\* This word (pretty) is used to describe people ("pretty girl") but not objects (not "pretty flower," or "pretty dress").*

## *Now try making a few simple sentences using the words above*

_____

_____

_____

_____

_____

---

### WORD BANK

'E'AL, FN<u>AWE</u>', HIYÌK, KALIN, KEF<u>TX</u>O, KÌ'O<u>NG</u>, K<u>LL</u>V<u>AW</u>M, KU'UP, LEH<u>AW</u><u>NG</u>, LESAR,

LETAM, MUN<u>TX</u>A, <u>NG</u>ÄZÌK, <u>PX</u>ASUL, S<u>AY</u>RÌP, SEVIN, SKIEN, S<u>TX</u>O<u>NG</u>, SYÄ'Ä, Y<u>AY</u>MAK

# Na'vi Mystery Word Puzzles

**These are really easy, once you get the hang of them.** The mystery word is missing. <u>In its place we have put the exact number of boxes as it has letters.</u> For example, if the Na'vi mystery word were Irayo *(Thank you)*, there would be 4 boxes (I R AY O). To figure out the mystery word, simply fill in the missing letter from each "clue word" below, and write it in the appropriate box. In the puzzle below, the word in clue #1 ("___ T A N") is missing its first letter. So, you simply write in the missing letter and then in box #1 (which corresponds to "clue #1") you write that same letter. For clue #2, you would put the missing letter in box #2, and so on. **Hint:** Start with the words you know. Be sure to fill in the missing letter both in the clue, and in the mystery word box. You may end up solving the mystery word before you solve all of the clues. If that happens, simply <u>go back to the clue words you are having trouble with</u>, and write in the missing letter, using the letter from the mystery word.

We have done the first puzzle for you to ensure you get the concept.

## Sample Puzzle

Na'vi word:

| ¹A | ²T | ³O | ⁴K | ⁵I | ⁶R | ⁷I | ⁸N | ⁹A | ¹⁰ | ' |
|---|---|---|---|---|---|---|---|---|---|---|

English word equivalent: *Very pure spirits/Seeds of the sacred tree*

| | | | |
|---|---|---|---|
| 1. _A_ T A N | *(light – opposite of dark)* | 6. _R_ EW O N | *(Morning)* |
| 2. E L _T_ U S I! | *(Hey! Pay attention! Stay focused!)* | 7. M _I_ P | *(New)* |
| 3. I R AY _O_ | *(Thanks!)* | 8. M E _N_ A R I | *(Eyes – specifically two eyes or a pair of)* |
| 4. _K_ A L TX Ì | *(Hello)* | 9. _A_ L A K S I | *(Ready)* |
| 5. K _I_ N Ä | *("7" – the number seven)* | 10. _'_ EY L A N | *(Friend)* |

## Puzzle 1 — Easy!

Na'vi phrase:

English phrase equivalent: _____

| | | | |
|---|---|---|---|
| 1. ___ A N | *(Blue)* | 4. ___ T R A L | *(Tree)* |
| 2. H O ___ | *(Few)* | 5. H A ___ EY | *(Done, or finished)* |
| 3. ___ Ì NG | *(Give)* | 6. H Ì ' ___ | *(Tiny – small in size)* |

18

## Puzzle 2 — Easy!

Na'vi phrase:

| 1 | 2 | 3 | ■ | 4 | 5 | 6 | 7 | 8 | 9 |
|---|---|---|---|---|---|---|---|---|---|

English word equivalent: _____

| | | | |
|---|---|---|---|
| 1. ___ O M P A | (Rain) | 6. ___ A L TX Ì | (Hello) |
| 2. S ___ | (And) | 7. ___ O M | (Eat) |
| 3. NG AW _____ | (Worm) | 8. Y ___ R | (Wash) |
| 4. ___ I P | (New) | 9. W I ___ | (Fast) |
| 5. N ___ Ä | (Grab) | | |

## Puzzle 3 — Easy!

Na'vi word:

| 1 | 2 | 3 | 4 | 5 | 6 | 7 | 8 | 9 |
|---|---|---|---|---|---|---|---|---|

English word equivalent: _____ *important* _____

| | | | |
|---|---|---|---|
| 1. F W E ___ | (Broken) | 6. M U ___ E | (2 – or "Two") |
| 2. TX ___ P | (Fire) | 7. A ___ A N | (Light) |
| 3. ___ E ' A | (See, physical sense) | 8. S ___ T | (Now) |
| 4. ___ U TX E | (Please) | 9. K I ___ | (Need) |
| 5. F T ___ NG | (Stop) | | |

## Puzzle 4 — Easy!

Na'vi phrase:

| 1 | 2 | 3 | ■ | 4 | 5 | 6 | 7 | ■ | 8 | 9 | 10 | 11 |
|---|---|---|---|---|---|---|---|---|---|---|----|----|

English phrase equivalent: _____

| | | | |
|---|---|---|---|
| 1. ' ___ ' | (Exciting) | 6. N ___ Ä | (Grab) |
| 2. TS ___ O | (Art) | 7. EY ___ T A N | (Leader, or boss) |
| 3. V U ___ | (Branch) | 8. S R ___ K | * (Marker for yes/no question) |
| 4. S KX A W ___ | (Idiot, moron) | 9. O M U ___ | (Know, understand) |
| 5. S R ___ N E | (Yes) | 10. K ___ H E | (No) |
| 11. K LL ___ E | (Ground – dirt, soil) | | |

*\* As explained on the page, "Srak?" the word srak comes after a sentence such as "Do you like pizza srak?" (Do you like pizza, yes/no?) <u>It shows that you are expecting</u> a "yes" or "no" from the other person.*

# Quotation Puzzle Fun!

*"My nose is full of his alien smell."*

Quotation puzzles are lots of fun, and quite easy once you get the hang of them.

We started this first one to help you understand how the process works. Fill in the quote (above) with the letters below. *BUT – the letters below are arranged in alphabetical order in each column. (a, o, u... e, h...)*

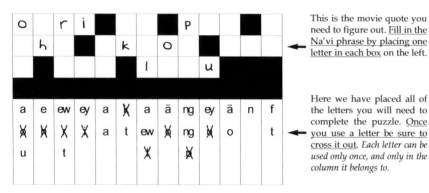

This is the movie quote you need to figure out. Fill in the Na'vi phrase by placing one letter in each box on the left.

Here we have placed all of the letters you will need to complete the puzzle. Once you use a letter be sure to cross it out. *Each letter can be used only once, and only in the column it belongs to.*

*"These demons are forbidden here."*

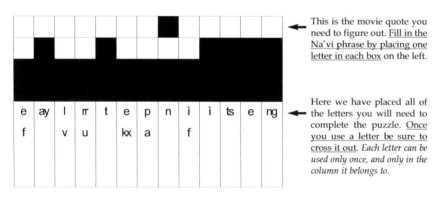

This is the movie quote you need to figure out. Fill in the Na'vi phrase by placing one letter in each box on the left.

Here we have placed all of the letters you will need to complete the puzzle. Once you use a letter be sure to cross it out. *Each letter can be used only once, and only in the column it belongs to.*

*"I have passed the tests. I respectfully request the Dream Hunt."*

20

# More Quotation Puzzles

*"Eytukan, I have something to say, to everyone. The words are like stones in my heart."*

* PLEASE NOTE: Late in the editing phase we realized that *ireiuo* (from James Cameron) was changed (by USC Professor Paul Frommer) to *irayo*. Simply put: **this book has taken three months out of my life** and I just found this book may not even see the light of day until FOX's lawyers decide "if" we can help you learn Na'vi for free. This puzzle takes too much effort to fix at this point, as no one is getting paid for any of this and no one may ever even be allowed to read this book. So these two grid squares are now fused together. I apologize for any inconvenience.

| ay | a | e | ' | l | a | ' | an | ay | r | a | e | o | m | e |
| m | l | ì | ' | l | ì | k | a |  | f | s | kx | p |  | ì |
| r | t |  | ay | t | u | n | u |  |  | l | u |  |  | r |
| u |  |  | ey | u |  | n |  |  |  |  |  |  |  |  |

*"A great evil is upon us. The Sky People are coming to destroy Hometree. They will be here soon."*

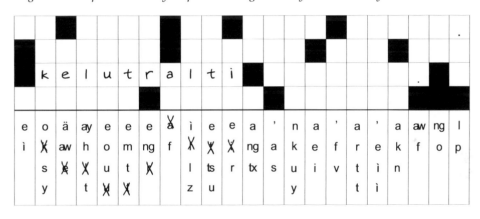

| e | o | ä | ay | e | e | e | ä | ì | e | e | a | ' | n | a | ' | a | ' | a | aw | ng | l |
| i | ✗ | aw | h | o | m | ng | f | ✗ | ✗ | ✗ | ng | a | k | e | f | r | e | k | f | o | p |
| s | ✗ | ✗ | u | t | ✗ |  | l | ts | r | tx | s | u | i | v | t | ì | n | f |  |  |  |
| y |  | t | ✗ | ✗ |  |  | z | u |  |  | y |  |  | t |  | ì |  |  |  |  |  |

*"I See you Brother, and thank you.*
*Your spirit goes with Eywa, your body stays behind to become part of the People."*

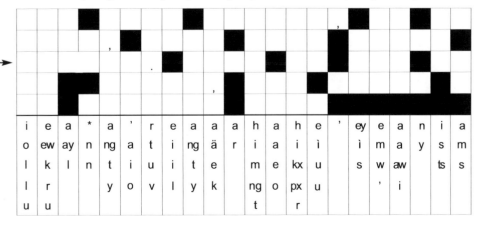

| i | e | a | * | a | ' | r | e | a | a | a | h | a | h | e | ' | ey | e | a | n | i | a |
| o | ew | ay | n | ng | a | t | i | ng | ä | r | i | a | i | ì |  | ì | m | a | y | s | m |
| l | k | l |  | t | u | i | t | e |  | m | e | kx | u |  | s | w | aw |  |  | ts | s |
| l | r |  |  | y | o | v | l | y | k |  | ng | o | px | u |  | ' | i |  |  |  |  |
| u | u |  |  |  |  |  |  |  |  |  | t | r |  |  |  |  |  |  |  |  |  |

# Quickie Cryptograms

Cryptograms are codes where one letter replaces another (hint: **A** *is really* **ts** below). Simply decipher the Na'vi words. (Easy, right?) To help, we have included the English equivalent word in parentheses below each word. <u>Once you have figured out a letter</u> in a Na'vi word, <u>that letter will be the same in all other Na'vi words</u> in this puzzle. The point of cryptograms is to get you used to recognizing digraphs (*ay, ey, kx, ng, ts, tx,* etc.) as <u>one letter</u>, or more correctly "**one symbol.**" Please take the time to do each of these. Start with the words you know.

## *Puzzle 1*

C V K G Ä M
*(Father)*

Q O E Z J
*(Mountain Banshee)*

I Z
*(You)*

B X B Ä B V
*(Sky Person)*

A Z K C Q U Ä
*(Warrior)*

Ì V ' M Z J
*(Heart)*

T Ö Z
*(Gaia/World Spirit)*

H V
*("I" or "me")*

A X O V
*(Sun)*

B H E Ä O
*(Last Shadow)*

A V H
*(Art)*

J Z J B Z I
*(Viperwolf)*

Q E W H
*(Thank You)*

B P S Ì T
*(Choice)*

K V J Z E Q
*(Pair of Eyes)*

A K Ä O Z J
*(Brother)*

O D
*(Time)*

C Z ' J H O
*(Mother)*

## *Puzzle 2*

A I Z M
*(Cup)*

N Z J P
*(Forbidden)*

Æ Ä M
*(Branch)*

Ì H J
*(Night)*

F Ä J
*(Arm)*

Ü Ä E
*(Wash)*

T Ö Z I Z R Ä
*(Polite Good Bye)*

F Ä J B Q M
*(Elbow)*

Ü H K
*(Eat)*

N T T
*(Error or Mistake)*

B D
*(Day)*

Ä Æ Z J
*(Game)*

O Z M Ì P
*(Hello)*

Æ W O D
*(Until)*

Ä B E Z M
*(Tree)*

A Z R T M Ä
*(Bond, or Neural connection)*

Ö H Ì
*(Whole)*

Å Z K Ä I V
*(Bring)*

# More Codes to Break

What fun are mind-bending puzzles if we don't include more? Not to worry the letter substitution code is the same in all four puzzles. The practice you get writing out each word as you break the code is more important than the actual breaking of the code itself.

## *Puzzle 3*

Å Ä G
*(Fall, or fall down)*

' Z K G Q
*(Touch)*

I Y Å P O
*(hard, or difficult – not "easy")*

Å P C P B
*(Year)*

T O
*(Lead – the action, not the metal)*

H R Z N
*(hungry)*

Å P C P O D
*(Season)*

T O B H J
*(Leader)*

G P Ö H F
*(Cloud)*

Ì Ä E
*(Strong)*

H M H ' T O B H J
*(Clan leader/Head honcho/Big kahuna)*

G L Ì V
*(Speak)*

N Z
*(Mouth)*

H J B Ä
*(Nose)*

G Y I N H
*(Chat)*

O L B V
*(Ground – what you stand on)*

I Y I
*(Stomach)*

Z F Z
*(Large)*

## *Puzzle 4*

T X E
*(right, or "correct")*

K L B V
*(Agree)*

Ì H J
*(Night)*

S Ì T
*(Choose)*

M D B H O
*(Smile)*

Æ D B V G
*(Demon)*

S Ì P
*(Tongue)*

K X T
*(Calm)*

Ü X J V
*(Beloved)*

R Z F P
*(Part)*

K T G
*(Weak)*

' U L
*(Plant)*

O V R V
*(No)*

J Z E Q
*(Eye)*

' T M Z J
*(Friend)*

M V R D Z G
*(Dangerous)*

I X I
*(Worm)*

Z B H O Q E Q J Z '
*(Seeds of the great tree)*

# Na'vi Letter Block

This is a crossword puzzle with a twist. Below you will find a block of letters. Each letter in that block appears <u>once</u>. Simply take each letter from the block and insert it in the crossword puzzle below. Make sure to cross it off once you use it. **To make this puzzle easier** we have included clues for each word in the puzzle below <u>and given you the first letter of each word</u>. *We even started the puzzle to get you going.* The solution may or may not appear at the end of the book.

## Clues:

| English equivalent | # of letters | 1st letter |
|---|---|---|
| And (this *and* that) | 2 | S |
| Agree | 4 | M |
| Ask | 3 | P |
| Ball | 3 | R |
| Blind | 6 | K |
| Bring | 6 | Z |
| Choose | 3 | F |
| Do, or make | 2 | S |
| Drink | 3 | N |
| Drop | 6 | T |
| Eat | 3 | Y |
| Jump | 3 | S |
| I get it/I understand | 6 | TS |
| Kiss | 3 | P |
| Know | 4 | O |
| Laugh | 6 | H |
| Lead | 2 | EY |
| Learn | 4 | N |
| Previous | 3 | H |
| Shadow | 2 | U |
| Shallow | 3 | R |
| Sound | 3 | P |
| Take, *or bring* | 4 | M |
| Teach | 3 | K |
| Thanks (or) Thank you | 4 | I |
| Think | 4 | F |
| This way!/Like this! | 5 | F |
| Tiny bit/Small amount | 3 | ' |
| Wash | 3 | Y |
| Wish | 5 | R |

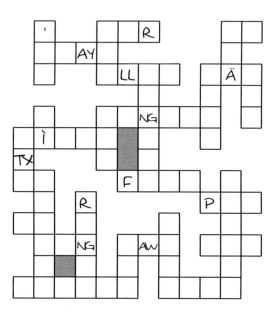

## Letter Block

| | | | | | | | | | |
|---|---|---|---|---|---|---|---|---|---|
| X́ | Ẍ | A | A | A | A | A | A | A | A |
| AW | AY | E | E | E | E | EY | X | F | F | H |
| H | I | I | Ì | X | K | K | K | L | L | X |
| M | M | M | M | M | M | M | M | N | X | NG |
| NG | NG | O | O | O | O | X | P | P | P | R | R |
| X | R | R | X | S | S | T | T | TS | X | U | U |
| U | U | U | U | U | U | Y | Y | Z | Z | ■ |

---

**WORD LIST:**

'IT, <u>EY</u>K, FÌFYA, FPÌL, F<u>TX</u> <u>EY</u>, HAM, HA<u>NG</u>HAM, IR<u>AY</u>O, KAKREL, KAR, M<u>LL</u>TE, MU<u>NGE</u>, NÄK, NUME, OMUM, PAM, P<u>AW</u>M, POM, RA<u>NG</u>AL, RE<u>NG</u>, RUM, SI, SÌ, SPÄ, <u>TS</u>LOLAM, TU<u>NG</u>ZUP, UK, YOM, YUR, ZAMU<u>NGE</u>

# The World Around You

In your day-to-day activities try replacing various words you use in English with their equivalent words in Na'vi. With a little practice you will find you have dozens, if not hundreds, of new words for things you see every day. This process of becoming familiar with basic Na'vi words will make learning advanced concepts like grammar and lenition *easy and stress-free.*

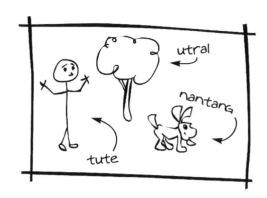

Flower   syulang

Petal   _____

Stem   _____

Leaf   rìk

Leaf   rìk

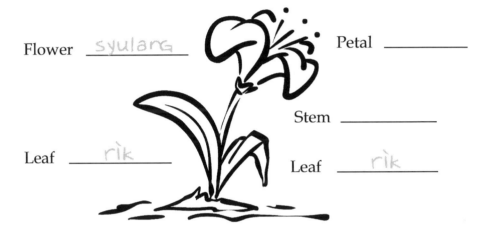

The Na'vi don't add an **"s"** to the end of a word to make it plural. <u>They add **"ay"** to the front of the word.</u> It's exactly the same as we do in English. It is just at the beginning of the word, like Pig-Latin.

Tree   utral

Many leaves   ayrìk

Branch   vul

Trunk   tangek

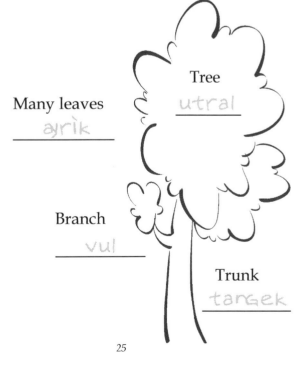

( . . . But not "hometree")

25

What do you tse'a?

*We wrote in the English words. You get to fill in the Na'vi words! Easy srak?*

Tree, or

_____

Leaves, or

_____

Sky, or

_____

Cloud, or

_____

Person, or

_____

Ground, or

_____

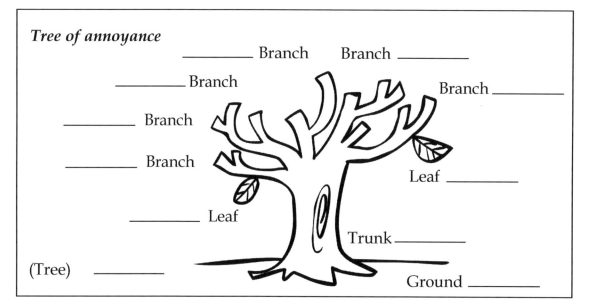

**Tree of annoyance**

_____ Branch    Branch _____

_____ Branch

_____ Branch        Branch _____

_____ Branch

Leaf _____

_____ Leaf

Trunk _____

(Tree) _____

Ground _____

# Sì versus ulte.

Both words mean "and," but sì connects two words (this **and** that—or this **sì** that). Ulte connects two clauses, or two sentences (We saw Avatar **and** then we ate dinner at the mall.—or—We saw Avatar **ulte** then we ate dinner at the mall.)

Please note, this lesson is not about grammar; it is simply about building vocabulary, so we are simply replacing "**and**" with "**sì**" or "**ulte**" as needed.

*Here are examples sentences using **sì** instead of **and**. Please write in **sì** in the blank spaces.*

For Christmas I got a bike, ____ a train, ____ an X-box, ____ some socks; but I don't count those.

Okay, I will have the cheeseburger, ____ some fries, ____ a Coke.

I have a brother ____ two sisters.

What have I been up to? Oh, this ____ that.

Okay, you . . . ____ you go over there. You two, ____ you as well stay here and set up camp.

Your girlfriend ____ her friend were here looking for you earlier.

*Here are examples sentences using **ulte** instead of **and**. Please write **ulte** in the blank spaces.*

Wash the dishes _____ while you are at it, feed the cat.

Okay, so our first stop is the Grand canyon _____ I want to buy some souvenirs for grandma.

Watch me _____ see if you can follow along.

If you doubt me, _____ I am sure that you do, you can verify the facts online.

After the game, _____ that means after your shower we can go; _____ you know what? I expect you to be on time _____ play your heart out _____ really try to win.

\* \* \*

Okay, so now we will use "**sì**" AND "**ulte**" in the following examples. If you get confused, we have included the answers at the bottom of the page in grey. Try not to look there unless you have to.

(Angry boss) "Hey! Stop goofing off ____ get back to work; ____ while you are at it work faster. I have a wife ____ kids to pay for, ____ a mortgage to pay."

(Bratty kid) "I want chocolate ice cream ____ vanilla ____ strawberry, wait—I don't like strawberry, _____ I want it in a cone, oh, _____ I want fudge ____ caramel all over it _____ peanuts too!"

\* \* \*

*(Angry boss) "Hey! Stop goofing off ULTE get back to work; ULTE while you are at it work faster. I have a wife SÌ kids to pay for, ULTE a mortgage to pay."*

*(Bratty kid) "I want chocolate ice cream SÌ vanilla SÌ strawberry, wait—I don't like strawberry, ULTE I want it in a cone, oh, ULTE I want fudge SÌ caramel all over it ULTE peanuts too!"*

# Na'vi Numbers

Humans have ten fingers (on average) and ten toes. This is why we count to ten, or use what scientists like to call a *"base-ten"* system of counting. Our <u>base</u> is ten. That is the foundation of our thinking. After we get to ten we simply mark off a little platform and start all over again. When we get to 100 (ten sets of ten) we mark off a big platform and start from one again. It is a nice way of keeping things simple.

But humans don't like simple. We really like to complicate things. That is why we have 7 ("not ten") days in a week, and 28, 29, 30 or 31 (also "not ten") days in a month, depending on our mood. Then we have 12 months in a year, 12 inches in a ruler; each inch is broken down into quarters and eighths, 3 feet in a yard, 8 notes on a musical scale, 52 cards in a deck . . .

Our *"base ten"* system is pretty fouled up when you think about it. Fortunately the Na'vi have no such problem. They have eight fingers and toes, so instead of counting to ten (1, 2, 3, 4, 5, 6, 7, 8, 9, 10) and starting all over again, they count to eight (1, 2, 3, 4, 5, 6, 7, 8) and start all over again. "8 is the new 10," just like *"50 (in human years) is the new 30,"* so it is said, and every year some new color is "the new black" in the fashion world. Humans can be really confusing and inconsistent.

But Na'vi numbers are nice and predictable. One through eight, *annnnnd* <u>stop</u>! Here's how it looks on paper—which the Na'vi don't have (more on that later).

## nìNa'vi:
*(that means "in Na'vi")*

## 1, 2, 3, 4, 5, 6, 7 – 8.

Let's get philosophical about this for a moment. When we count (in Earth numbers), each number is simply one step above the previous number. The distance traveled from 6 to 7 <u>is the same</u> as it is from *1 to 2*, or *9 to 10*, or *534 to 535*. The funky part is that when we go from nine to ten we tend to think of it as a set. We go from one digit to <u>two</u> digits. We make a little platform and plop a zero behind it. Visually it would look something like this:

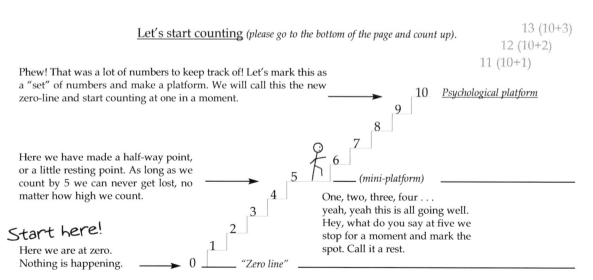

<u>Let's start counting</u> *(please go to the bottom of the page and count up).*

13 (10+3)
12 (10+2)
11 (10+1)

Phew! That was a lot of numbers to keep track of! Let's mark this as a "set" of numbers and make a platform. We will call this the new zero-line and start counting at one in a moment.

10   *Psychological platform*
9
8
7
6

Here we have made a half-way point, or a little resting point. As long as we count by 5 we can never get lost, no matter how high we count.

5   *(mini-platform)*

4

One, two, three, four . . .
yeah, yeah this is all going well.
Hey, what do you say at five we
stop for a moment and mark the
spot. Call it a rest.

3

2

**Start here!**

Here we are at zero.
Nothing is happening.

1

0   *"Zero line"*

What our ancestors have done in designing our current *"base ten"* numbering system is to make a process where non-mathematicians can easily handle large numbers without having the stress of mentally juggling various sets of data. Math is boring and reliable (just how we like it). Every five numbers we are half way to ten, and every ten numbers we have a "set."

It's just like money: *$1, $5, $10, $20, $50, $100.* Anyone can remember that. All derivatives of <u>ten</u>.

But when we start counting in Na'vi the *"base eight"* system makes our brains all scrambly. Suddenly ten is not 10, but "8 + 2," and 12 is 8.5, or *a set and a half.* <u>So we need to understand our basic philosophy of numbers</u> (which we just covered) so we can "think in Na'vi," instead of constantly trying to convert *10 to 8* and counting our fingers but not thumbs. When we are dealing with small numbers this is not an issue, but the moment we start working with larger numbers like 32 (8 x 4) and 75 (8 x 9 + 3) we can easily get frustrated and hopelessly confused.

<u>So let's look at the world in Na'vi math:</u>

<u>Let's start counting</u> (*ni'Na'vi* this time).

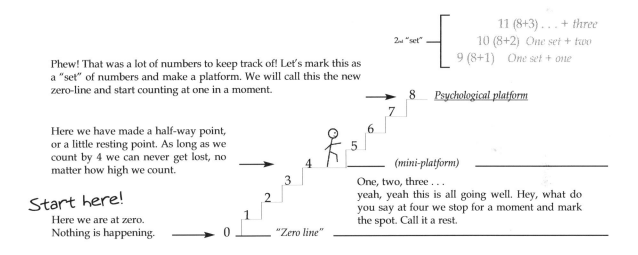

2ⁿᵈ "set"
11 (8+3) . . . + *three*
10 (8+2) *One set + two*
9 (8+1) *One set + one*

Phew! That was a lot of numbers to keep track of! Let's mark this as a "set" of numbers and make a platform. We will call this the new zero-line and start counting at one in a moment.

8  *Psychological platform*
7
6

Here we have made a half-way point, or a little resting point. As long as we count by 4 we can never get lost, no matter how high we count.

5
4  *(mini-platform)*
3

One, two, three . . .
yeah, yeah this is all going well. Hey, what do you say at four we stop for a moment and mark the spot. Call it a rest.

**Start here!**
Here we are at zero.
Nothing is happening.

2
1
0  *"Zero line"*

# "8 is the new 10"

Here is a pleasant little mind-bender: 1-8 = one *set* on Pandora. 1-10 = one *set* on Earth. One *set* is marked by a tally mark, or in modern ages, like the one we like to think we are in, we use the assigned digit (1, 2, 3, etc.) <u>to indicate the number of tally marks</u>, or number of sets. Instead of using |||| or ////, or even XXXX to mean "4 sets" we simply use the digit "40." On Earth, "40" is the modern Western symbol for forty individual pieces, or the equivalent count.

So by Pandoran standards 10 = 8 as 10 (the symbol "10", not the count "ten") indicates one set and "zero" additions. In Na'vi it could look like this, *if* the Na'vi ever decided to use written symbols, as they don't waste their time with artificial concepts like writing.

*Na'vi finger count: 1, 2, 3, 4, 5, 6, 7 – **10**  (One complete set)*
*"Earth numbers": 1, 2, 3, 4, 5, 6, 7 – **8***

11*, 12*, 13*, 14*, 15*, 16*, 17* – **20**  (Two complete sets)
9, 10, 11, 12, 13, 14, 15 – **16**  (Two complete sets)

Now the problem we have here is obvious. We are using Terran (Earth, or Sol |||) numbers *and* counting systems to base our argument on. 1-7 is easily enough translatable to Na'vi philosophy and 9-15 in a count form can be achieved, by using fingers and toes of either species. Our usage of the symbols 9-15 would be correct *ni'Na'vi* but wildly incomprehensible on Earth and lead to all kinds of numerical mismanagement. But **20** still means **16** on Pandora and Earth respectively.

*11 as in "<u>One set</u> plus one" or:vol+1, vol+2, vol+3, vol+4,vol+5,vol+6,vol+7,vol+vol (two sets – <u>now it's time to start counting tosies</u>).*

# Daisy chain words

Each Na'vi word in this exercise begins with the last letter of the previous word. This makes a giant daisy chain of words, which we have put in a nice "stair-step" order. All you have to do is figure out which Na'vi words go with each English word in the Word Bank below. Start with the words you know. In the example we have used two-letter words. In the exercise we will have you use three-letter words.

F U ___ _or_

U K _shadow_

K O _solicit agreement_

O E _I (or) me_

In the example puzzle on the left we have daisy-chained four 2-letter words together to make a simple stair-step pattern. Then we filled in the English equivalents of each word. In the puzzle below we have given you 3-letter words to play with. Please fill in each word's meaning in the spaces provided.

## In English:

_____

_____

_____

_____

_____

_____

_____

_____

_____

_____

_____

_____

## In Na'vi

'  AW M
    Ì
      N Ä K
        Ì
        NG AW NG
          EY
        N I Ä
          I
        E A N
          AW
          M AW EY
            AW
            R O L

---

**WORD LIST:**

'AWM = _____    MÌN = _____    NÄK = _____    KÌNG = _____

NGEYN = _____    NIÄ = _____    ÄIE = _____    EAN = _____

NAWM = _____    M AW EY = _____    EY AWR = _____    ROL = _____

# Na'vi Plurals

To make a word plural in English we often add an *s* at the end of the word; or *es*, depending on the word. For example cat becomes cats, horse becomes horses, clock becomes clocks, and fox becomes foxes. We will ignore the changing of words completely (*e.g. person becomes people, mouse becomes mice*) for the moment to avoid confusion. To get you used to the basic use of Na'vi plurals we will focus only on the similarity between the addition of an *s* (or *es*, as above) and the Na'vi use of *ay*.

The *s* you add to the end of a word in English to make it plural it is called a <u>suffix</u>. As suffix is the addition of a letter (or a few letters) to the <u>end</u> of a word.

<u>Example in English</u>: ikran*s*, or ikrans.

In Na'vi (or *nìNa'vi*) you would add *ay* to the beginning of a word to make it plural. This is called a <u>prefix</u>. Thus the simplest explanation is that in Na'vi (or "*nìNa'vi*") you will often use *ay* in front of a word instead of *s* at the end of a word. Please pardon the oversimplification, but once you grasp this concept and assimilate it, you will know it for life.

<u>Example nìNa'vi</u>: *ay*ikran, or ayikran.

Here are some practice exercises to help you remember the concept and build good Na'vi habits. Please fill in the blanks below:

| <u>Singular</u> *(in English)* | <u>Plural</u> *(in English)* | <u>Plural</u> *(nìNa'vi)* | <u>Singular</u> *(nìNa'vi)* |
|---|---|---|---|
| ikran | ikrans | ayikran | ikran |
| mountain | mountains | ayram | ram |
| leaf | leaves | ____rìk | rìk |
| _____ | balls | ____rum | rum |
| _____ | bodies | ____tokx | tokx |
| rock | _____ | ____tskxe | _____ |
| name | _____ | _____ | tstxo |
| night | _____ | _____ | txon |
| branch | _____ | _____ | vul |
| brain | _____ | _____ | eltu |
| _____ | feet | _____ | venu |

# Sudoku nì'Na'vi!

To help you master your Na'vi numbers we present some super-easy sudoku puzzles in Na'vi. You can fill them in using integers (1, 2, 3 . . .) or the Na'vi words for the numbers. Of course we recommend that you use the Na'vi words for numbers. Here are the numbers from one through nine *nì'Na'vi* to help you out: 'aw, mune, pxey, tsìng, mrr, pukap, kinä, vol, volaw. (*Solutions are at the back of the book*).

Ready srak? *kä!*

## Puzzle #1 *(easy)*

|       | tsìng |       | pxey  | vol   |       |       | mrr   | mune  |
|-------|-------|-------|-------|-------|-------|-------|-------|-------|
| 'aw   |       | mrr   |       | tsìng | pukap | kinä  | volaw |       |
| volaw |       | vol   |       | mrr   | mune  | pxey  | tsìng |       |
|       | pxey  |       | tsìng | pukap |       |       | 'aw   | vol   |
|       |       |       |       |       |       |       |       |       |
| vol   | mune  | tsìng |       |       | 'aw   | mrr   |       |       |
|       |       |       |       |       |       |       |       |       |
| kinä  | pukap | 'aw   |       |       | vol   | tsìng |       |       |

## Practice grid *(use this to solve the puzzle if you need)*

# More Na'vi Sudoku!

We hope you will enjoy Na'vi sudoku, but even if you are not a sudoku fan you can do these puzzles and practice your Na'vi numbers. Simply flip to the back of the book and pencil in each answer in these two puzzles. After your have written each Na'vi number word write in the digit the word represents. This practice will help you remember Na'vi numbers easier.

## Puzzle #2 *(easy)*

| | | mune | | 'aw | tsìng | mrr | pukap | |
| --- | --- | --- | --- | --- | --- | --- | --- | --- |
| | | mrr | | | pxey | | 'aw | mune |
| | | tsìng | | | | kinä | pxey | |
| | | | | mune | kinä | | | |
| mune | | | | vol | volaw | | | |
| | | 'aw | pxey | mrr | | | | |
| 'aw | | | | | | vol | mrr | |
| vol | mrr | kinä | | | | | mune | pxey |
| pxey | | | | | | | | tsìng |

## Practice grid *(use this to solve the puzzle if you need)*

# Things you can do with a friend

This is is an exercise in simple word substitution. We will use English as our base language and simply replace certain words with words in Na'vi. As this is a super-easy exercise designed to get you started down the path of learning Na'vi we will not be worrying about things like grammar at this moment.

The point of this particular exercise is to give you some practice writing out Na'vi words in the actual context of conversation. In following volumes we will be much more particular about tenses, lenition, and so on. Right now we just want to get those hands moving in concert with your optic and cranial functioning.

Here are some thing you can do with a friend. Simply fill in the Na'vi words*. We have shaded in the actual Na'vi words lightly. Take your pen or pencil and write over the letters. This will help cement the Na'vi words into your subconscious. These are the first of many baby steps and while this may seem too easy to have any lasting value these steps will greatly accelerate your assimilation of the Na'vi language in your daily awareness. *So let's do this:*

NGA can YOM a hot dog (or a tofu dog if you are a vegetarian). "YOM YOM YOM !"
*(You)* *(eat)* *(eat)* *(eat)* *(eat)*

NGA might PAWM OE to SRUNG SI you TÄFTXU a new hammock to HAHAW in.
*(You)* *(ask)* *(me)* *(help)* *(weave)* *(sleep)*

NGA can PENG them to ELTU SI and SRUNG SI you YUR your new hammock.
*(You)* *(tell)* *(stop goofing off)* *(help)* *(wash)*

## See? Friends are good for lots of things!

A good bribe is to PÄNU to KAR them how to MAKTO a PA'LI for helping you YUR
*(promise)* *(teach)* *(ride)* *(dire horse)* *(wash)*

and TÄFTXU your MIP hammock. You can even HAHAW with your AYEYLAN in your
*(weave)* *(new)* *(sleep)* *(friends)*

MIP hammock, as Na'vi are very communal and HAHAW together in APXA hammocks.
*(new)* *(sleep)* *(large)*

Why not KÄ to KELUTRAL and NUME PXAY AYSREW with your EYLAN ?
*(go)* *(Hometree)* *(learn)* *(many)* *(dances)* *(friend)*

After all of this activity, NGA may want to HUM and PENG your 'EYLAN that NGA are
*(you)* *(leave)* *(tell)* *(friend)* *(you)*

going to HAHAW . PAWM them to deliver a UPXARE to your SEMPUL or SA'NOK.
*(sleep)* *(Ask)* *(message)* *(father)* *(mother)*

# Happy Fun Page!

Learning a new language is *hard!* Well, we hope you are having fun with <u>this</u> workbook and that it is not too hard for you. But just to make sure you are not overly stressed out with cramming your *eltu* with too many new words and exotic phrases we have intentionally left this page blank. You can use to doodle some Pandoran art, or make a list of Na'vi words you know without having to look them up, or design your own puzzle, or just write hate mail to the author. *Explore your creativity!* **Ready srak?**

# Na'vi Gingerbread Anatomy

Brain _____

*(we're assuming it's in there somewhere)\**

Head _____

Eyes *(both)* _____

Nose _____

Mouth _____

Hand _____

Finger _____
*(Hmm . . . not so much)*

Knee _____

Foot _____

_____ Eye *(just one)*

_____ Ear *(it's there somewhere)*

_____ Arm

_____ Elbow

_____ Tail *(you can't see it)*

_____ Leg

_____ Toe

*(Yeah, we have never seen a gingerbread man with a toe either)*

*\* (No one is THAT happy all of the time)*

---

# Mini Na'vi anatomy reverse criss-cross

This time we have filled in this puzzle for you but left the clues unanswered. The words in this puzzle exactly match the words you need in the puzzle above. Here we have provided the Na'vi words.

## ACROSS

3. re'o _____
5. menari _____
6. nari _____
7. kxa _____
8. tsyokx _____
10. zekwä _____
11. pxun _____
12. venzek _____
14. kinamtil _____

## DOWN

1. venu _____
2. kinam _____
4. ontu _____
5. mikyun _____
9. kxetse _____
11. pxuntil _____
13. eltu _____

### Hints:

**ACROSS**

3. *You bump things with this.*
5. *These give you depth perception.*
6. *I spy, with my brown _____ . . .*
7. *You have one of these for a reason.*
8. *_____ me that plate please.*
10. *Stop poking me with that!*
11. *My what a strong _____ you have.*
12. *Some people have a _____ fetish.*
14. *These often require pads.*

**DOWN**

1. *Athletes get this.*
2. *Jake's didn't work.*
4. *Roses seduce this.*
5. *You have two of these for a reason.*
9. *If you had one of these . . .*
11. *This has a funny bone.*
14. *Think, man! Think!*

# Srak?

*Srak* is a fun word. <u>You add it to the end of a statement or direct question</u> in Na'vi (or "*nì'Na'vi*") to tell your listener(s) <u>that you are looking for a yes or no</u> answer from them. If you were to try this in English it would be something akin to adding "*, right?*" at the end of a statement to solicit agreement or as part of a question directly asking for confirmation or denial. **Also, use srak in all yes/no questions:**

## *Here are a few examples:*

"You put that there srak?" *(or roughly equivalent to "You put that there, didn't you?")*

"Did you wash your hands for dinner srak?"

"Coming srak?" *(or "Are you coming along?" or it's shortened version "Coming?")*

"The sawtute vrrtep have decimated our homeland srak?" *(Here srak is used to solicit agreement)*

And finally . . . "You can't buy a better ikran anywhere than Crazy Al's, srak?"*
*(\* Here the salesman is leading the prospect, trying to elicit subconscious buying patterns.)*

❖   ❖   ❖

For each question below, please put a question mark at the end of each sentence below, or write **srak** *followed by a question mark,* as you feel best. Only questions below that ask for a yes/no response need "srak" added at the end of the sentence.

1. Is this the first question _____

2. Are you enjoying the time and effort you are investing in Learning the Na'vi language _____

3. Avatar rocked _____ (was very enjoyable to watch)

4. What else would you like to learn about the Na'vi _____

5. Where do you think Toruk flew off to at the end of the movie _____

6. Toruk was big, red, and dangerous _____

7. Doing crosswords in Na'vi is challenging, don't you think _____

8. How you do something is more important than how fast it is done _____

9. How do you do something fast if it is not important to get done _____

10. Would you be interested in a second volume of this series that deals with grammar _____

11. Ready to learn some grammar _____

12. Did you finish the giant crossword puzzle yet _____

13. What is your favorite Avatar website _____

14. Have you listened to the Radio Avatar podcasts yet _____

15. Do you want YouTube instructional videos _____

16. What are your ideas to make learning Na'vi easier _____

17. What kind of Na'vi comic do we need to help us learn _____

18. This can't go on any longer, as there is no more room on the page, is there _____

# Wait, wait!! — "Who?" "What?" "Where?"

In English we have the five classic question words: **"who, what, when, where, and why."**

. . . Oh, and how, so that makes six. 6 classic question words.

<u>Na'vi simplifies all of that</u>: We have **"what."** Sounds exciting--right?

Well, once you get to know it, it actually is! You see, once you know the root word for "what" you can figure out (what) to attach it to, depending on (what) you want to ask.

What--person ("Who"): tu<u>pe</u> "Who/**Tupe** ate my donut?!!"

What--thing ("What"): '<u>upe</u> "What/**'upe** is that you're eating?" *(A donut?)*

What--action ("What"): kem<u>pe</u> "What/**Kempe** are you doing?!"

What--time ("When"): kɾɾ<u>pe</u> "Exactly when/**Kɾɾpe** did I give your permission to yom my donut?"

What--place ("Where"): tseng<u>pe</u> "Where/**Tsengpe** did you get that donut mister?"

What--reason ("Why"): lum<u>pe</u> "Why/**Lumpe** did you think you could yom my donut?"

What--way, manner, or method ("How"): fya<u>pe</u> "How/**Fyape** did you plan on getting away with this criminal act?"

## *Did you notice all of the pe's?*

That is the commonality, <u>the root to look for</u>. It can appear at the beginning or the end of the word (fyape or pefya). Example:

**Tseng** is defined as "<u>place</u>" in the dictionary. Tsengpe is "<u>what</u> place?" or "where?" *See?* It all fits together.

Try thinking of Na'vi as a modular language *(like a modular house--where pieces are pre-formed and you can mix and match **pre-made** windows and walls and roofs to design your custom house).* You have a ready made word <u>and you can alter it</u>. The Chinese language has a word for everything, *but no plurals* I am led to believe. But that is a LOT of words to learn. The English language changes some words *(run becomes ran in the past tense)* but it also has completely different words *(eat becomes ate — not very modular).* Na'vi gives you a lot of base words you can add prefixes or suffixes to, or even infixes *(as in: "inside the word" -fixes).*

<u>This is a generality</u> and not an authoritative diatribe on everything Na'vi. But thinking about it this way will help you a LOT in learning new words, and understanding how the whole grammar thing works. In volumes 2, 3, and 4 this will all be examined and cleared up gently and easily, with no harsh study guidelines and stress-free methods to facilitate retention.

**If we tried to teach you <u>everything at once</u> you would not remember any of it 3 months from now.** <u>That is where most instruction in Na'vi has been failing to this point</u>, *and continues to lose students.*

# Na'vi Categories

This puzzle simply asks you to <u>look at the words below and assign them to the categories you think they fit in</u>. Of course we would like you to also write in the translations (English word equivalents) in the spaces to the right of each word. **Each word in each row will begin with the same letter** (which we have provided in the left column).

|   | Actions | Animals | Body Parts | People |
|---|---------|---------|------------|--------|
| S |         |         |            |        |
| P |         |         |            |        |
| E |         |         |            |        |
| N |         |         |            |        |
| T |         |         |            |        |

WORD LIST:

Eltu _____

Eltungawng _____

Eyk _____

Eyktan _____

Nantang _____

Nari _____

Nga _____

Nume _____

Pa'li _____

Plltxe _____

Poe _____

Pxun _____

Sempul _____

Seyri _____

Srew _____

Swirä _____

Taronyu _____

Tawng _____

Toruk _____

Txìm _____

*In 3 minutes scribble as many Na'vi words (that are not on this page) as you know.*

# Everyday words in Na'vi

To solve this puzzle, you will need to fill in the sentences below with the Na'vi equivalent word *(we have provided you with the English equivalent word in parentheses to help)*. Then write that word in the puzzle. Sounds pretty simple <u>srak</u>? **Here's a hint though:** The puzzle tells you how many letters are in the Na'vi word you are looking for. We have filled in one answer to help get you started and if you need additional help we have included a word bank at the bottom of the page. Also, the solution appears at the end of the book. Good luck!

## ACROSS

1. This _____ you should learn Na'vi. Next _____, French.
   *(year)* *(year)*
5. "A _____ in the hand" is not worth as much as an ikran.
   *(bird)*
7. You see with your _____. I "see" with my heart.
   *(eye)*
8. To become clan-member you must first pass the _____.
   *(test)*
10. _____ me back my toy ikran or I am telling mom!
    *(Give)*
11. You _____ ikran! You _____ a faster way to travel!
    *(need)* *(need)*
12. _____ me to this tawtute you have found.
    *(Lead)*
13. I ate too many brainworms (*ayeltungawng*)! I am _____!
    *(full)*
14. You're asking _____? _____ don't know. _____ am lost.
    *(me)* *(I)* *(I)*
15. You should _____ your bike to work. Save the planet.
    *(ride)*
16. Now, I will do this _____, and only _____, srak?
    *(once)* *(once)*
17. One _____ please. I need a _____ to gather my thoughts.
    *(moment)* *(moment)*
18. The evil space fish swam away with my arrow _____!
    *(again)*

## DOWN

2. Ow! I cut my _____ on that stupid helicoradian (*lorayu*) plant.
   *(lip)*
3. _____! Yes _____ over there! What mischief are _____ up to?
   *(You)* *(you)* *(you)*
4. Aynantang (*viperwolves*) are great pets. They _____ anything you toss.
   *(chase)*
5. You (*nga*) should _____ before we go. We may not _____ later.
   *(eat)* *(eat)*
6. Oh, you gotta ask the _____ about that.
   *(chief – boss – clan leader)*
7. Only by _____ resisting RDA encroachment can any of us be free.
   *(continually)*
8. The way he is swinging that branch you had better _____ or you will get bonked.
   *(duck)*
9. Ooh! The _____ one! Win me (*oe*) the _____ one!
   *(blue)* *(blue)*
10. _____ some of us don't feel the need to show up on time.
    *(Apparently)*
11. Do _____ tempt me. Do _____ even think about it right now.
    *(not)* *(not)*
15. I am _____. I am _____ and at peace. Don't worry about me.
    *(calm)* *(calm)*
17. Okay, you _____ you, _____ . . . you get to play with the ikran.
    *(and)* *(and)*

In the movie, the word Neytiri used was <u>*mawey,*</u> but she used it to tell people to "calm down!"

*"Tam tam"* is the word to tell someone to "be calm." Mawey is an ajective (a state of being; "I am calm") not a verb (action; "Calm down!").

On a sie note: In the movie Neytiri tells Seze, "Tam tam," as she soothes her ikran.

## WORD BANK

<u>Across:</u> *'awlo, eyk, kin, makto, nari, nìmum, oe, swaw, taya, tìfmetok, tìng, yayo, zìsìt*

<u>Down:</u> *ean, fawi, ke, mawey, nga, nìtut, olo'eyktan, seyri, sì, tatlam, tawng, yom*

40

# Diametrical opposites

This    That

Below are words lined up in two columns. Simply draw a line from one word to its most appropriate opposite on the other side of the page. Given that we are working with a language that is still in development, these words may or may not be exact opposites, so choose the most appropriate word in your opinion. Don't forget to write in the English translations! Good luck!

| | | | |
|---|---|---|---|
| _____ | TRR | SÌLTSAN | _____ |
| _____ | FÌ'U | NGA | _____ |
| _____ | NA'VI | TAWTUTE | _____ |
| _____ | ALÌM | TSMUKAN | _____ |
| _____ | SEMPUL | TUTAN | _____ |
| _____ | KAWNG | HUM | _____ |
| _____ | PÄHEM | TSA'U | _____ |
| _____ | TERKUP | KEHE | _____ |
| _____ | TUTE | SA'NOK | _____ |
| _____ | OE | TXON | _____ |
| _____ | NGAY | TSLENG | _____ |
| _____ | SRANE | ASIM | _____ |
| _____ | TSMUKE | REY | _____ |

# Na'vi Mystery Word Puzzles

## (Part two)

Same rules apply (see "Na'vi Mystery Word Puzzles" earlier in the book) except that now we want you to <u>use each word in a sentence</u>. This is still simple word substitution so there should be no stress at all. But we want you to get in the habit of thinking nì'Na'vi *(in Na'vi)* so that in the next volume, when we start to incorporate grammar and other fun linquistic concepts you will have a much easier time making sense of it all. So let's have some fun with this, srak?

## Sample Puzzle

Na'vi word:

| ¹N | ²U | ³M | ⁴TS | ⁵E | ⁶NG |
|----|----|----|-----|----|-----|

English word equivalent: <u>school</u>

| | |
|---|---|
| 1. K I <u>N</u>  *(need)* | "I <u>kin</u> you to do this for me." |
| 2. R <u>U</u> M *(ball)* | "You will never get that <u>rum</u> away from the dog." |
| 3. S O <u>M</u> *(hot)* | "Don't touch that—it's <u>som</u>!" |
| 4. <u>TS</u> E O *(art)* | "This requires a delicate touch. It is more <u>tseo</u> than science." |
| 5. <u>E</u> L T U *(brain)* | "You need a bigger <u>eltu</u>. You sound like a sawtute." |
| 6. S R U <u>NG</u> *(help – or – assistance)* | "That is too heavy; you should get some <u>srung</u> with that." |

Now use the mystery word in a sentence: <u>If there was a Na'vi numtseng, would you go?</u>

## Puzzle 5 — Easy!

Na'vi phrase:

| ¹ | ² | ³ | ■ | ⁴ | ⁵ | ⁶ |
|---|---|---|---|---|---|---|

English phrase equivalent: <u>calm—be content—there there</u>

| | | | |
|---|---|---|---|
| 1. ___ RR | *(Day)* | " | " |
| 2. H ___ Y | *(Next)* | " | " |
| 3. ___ RR | *(Five)* | " | " |
| 4. ___ AW | *(Sky)* | " | " |
| 5. H ___ M | *(Previous)* | " | " |
| 6. ___ EY P | *(Weak)* | " | " |

Now use the mystery word in a sentence: _____

# Puzzle 6 — Easy!

Na'vi word:

| 1 | 2 | 3 | 4 | 5 | 6 |
|---|---|---|---|---|---|
|   |   |   |   |   |   |

English word equivalent: _slowly_

| 1. ___ EW *(Want)* | " | " |
|---|---|---|
| 2. F TX ___ *(Tongue)* | " | " |
| 3. S ___ X AW NG *("One who does not see")*\* | " | " |
| 4. ___ AW L O *(Once)* | " | " |
| 5. ___ L O ' *(Clan)* | " | " |
| 6. NG AW ___ *(Worm)* | " | " |

*(\* Moron – not blind person)*

Now use the mystery word in a sentence: _____

# Puzzle 7 — Not quite as easy

Na'vi word:

| 1 | 2 | 3 | 4 | 5 | 6 | 7 | 8 |
|---|---|---|---|---|---|---|---|
|   |   |   |   |   |   |   |   |

English word equivalent: _passion_

| 1. ___ Ì K AW NG | *(Evil)* | " | " |
|---|---|---|---|
| 2. P ___ W O PX | *(Cloud)* | " | " |
| 3. F Ì ___ Y A | *("This way" – "like this")* | " | " |
| 4. R U ___ E | *(Please)* | " | " |
| 5. N ___ R I | *(Eye)* | " | " |
| 6. ___ E N U | *(Foot)* | " | " |
| 7. ' ___ M P I | *(Touch)* | " | " |
| 8. N A N T A ___ | *(Viperwolf)* | " | " |

Now use the mystery word in a sentence: _____

You may have noticed that in these puzzles we are including words we have not already covered in previous exercises.

These exercises and puzzles are designed to allow you to find the answers by using any of a few diferent clues, but if you find any words to be too dificult simply flip to the back of the book and look through either of our word lists. You will find a basic word list in English and in Na'vi. If you require the latest copy of the Na'vi dictionaries you can find the links at the back of the book as well.

## Puzzle 8 — Not quite as easy

Na'vi word:

| 1 | 2 | 3 | 4 | 5 |
|---|---|---|---|---|
|   |   |   |   |   |

English word equivalent: _married (or "mated")_

| | | |
|---|---|---|
| 1. K Ì Y E V A ___ E  *(Goodbye)* | " | " |
| 2. ___ T R A L  *(Tree)* | " | " |
| 3. K I L V A ___  *(River)* | " | " |
| 4. ___ A M P AY  *(Ocean)* | " | " |
| 5. P AY F Y ___  *(Stream)* | " | " |

Now use the mystery word in a sentence: _____

## Puzzle 9 — Hard

Na'vi word:

| 1 | 2 | 3 | 4 | 5 | 6 | 7 | 8 |
|---|---|---|---|---|---|---|---|
|   |   |   |   |   |   |   |   |

English word equivalent:

_spelling (noun)_

| | | |
|---|---|---|
| 1. U T R A L TS Y Ì ___ *(Bush)* | " | " |
| 2. KX ___  *(Mouth)* | " | " |
| 3. H A ___  *(Previous)* | " | " |
| 4. S ___ E W  *(Dance)* | " | " |
| 5. K ___ W  *(0 – or"Zero")* | " | " |
| 6. ___ U  *(Is)* | " | " |
| 7. ___ U  *(Or)* | " | " |
| 8. ___ EY  *(Straight)* | " | " |
| 9. Y ___  *(Air)* | " | " |

Now use the mystery word in a sentence: _____

---

### Na'vi Connect-the-dots!

Yeah, yeah, it's a kid's puzzle. <u>But it is a great way to help you remember</u> the words for the numbers 1-8 in Na'vi.

After you connect the dots write the Na'vi words for each number.

kew •          • vol
'aw •   XXXX   • kinä
mune •  XXXX   • pukap
pxey •   • mrr

tsìng •

| | |
|---|---|
| Zero | _____ |
| One | _____ |
| Two | _____ |
| Three | _____ |
| Four | _____ |
| Five | _____ |
| Six | _____ |
| Seven | _____ |
| Eight | _____ |

## Puzzle 10 — Hard

Na'vi word:

| 1 | 2 | 3 | 4 | 5 | 6 | 7 | 8 | 9 | 10 |
|---|---|---|---|---|---|---|---|---|----|
|   |   |   |   |   |   |   |   |   |    |

English word equivalent:

*harmony – living at one with nature*

| | | |
|---|---|---|
| 1. V AW ___ | *(Dark)* | " " |
| 2. TS ___ O | *(Art)* | " " |
| 3. W ___ K | *(Loud)* | " " |
| 4. P AY O___ NG | *(Fish)* | " " |
| 5. V ___ R | *(Story)* | " " |
| 6. W I ___ | *(Fast)* | " " |
| 7. ' E V ___ | *(Kid – affectionate term)* | " " |
| 8. A T ___ N | *(Light – noun)* | " " |
| 9. F T U ___ | *(Easy, or simple)* | " " |
| 10. F T ___ NG | *(Stop)* | " " |

Now use the mystery word in a sentence: _____

## Puzzle 11 — Hard

Na'vi word:

| 1 | 2 | 3 | 4 | 5 | 6 | ■ | 7 | 8 | 9 | 10 | 11 | 12 |
|---|---|---|---|---|---|---|---|---|---|----|----|----|
|   |   |   |   |   |   |   |   |   |   |    |    |    |

English word equivalent:

*science*

| | | |
|---|---|---|
| 1. ___ AW | *(Sky)* | " " |
| 2. S ___ | *(And)* | " " |
| 3. ___ N U | *(Quiet – verb)* | " " |
| 4. ___ RR | *(Day)* | " " |
| 5. S ___ | *(Do)* | " " |
| 6. H ___ | *(So, or "in that case")* | " " |
| 7. U ___ | *(Shadow)* | " " |
| 8. K ___ N | *(Need)* | " " |
| 9. ___ Ì T RR | *(Today)* | " " |
| 10. F ___ EW | *(Mighty)* | " " |
| 11. ' ___ NG | *(Respond – verb)* | " " |
| 12. S L ___ | *(But)* | " " |

Now use the mystery word in a sentence: _____

**Please note:** *All of these words appear in this workbook. Most of them you have already used.*

# Puzzle 12 — Hard

**Na'vi word:**

| 1 | 2 | 3 | 4 | 5 | 6 | 7 |
|---|---|---|---|---|---|---|
|   |   |   |   |   |   |   |

**English word equivalent:** _____

*(Hint: Found only on Pandora)*

| | | |
|---|---|---|
| 1. K ___ | (____) | "   " |
| 2. ___ U | (____) | "   " |
| 3. ___ O KX | (_____) | "   " |
| 4. ' ___ | (_____) | "   " |
| 5. TXÌ ____ | (_____) | "   " |
| 6. H A H ____ | (_____) | "   " |
| 7. S R U ____ | (_____) | "   " |

Now use the mystery word in a sentence: _____

# Puzzle 13 — Ngäzìk — *RDA Corporate approved*

**Na'vi Phrase: "** _____ **."**

| 1 | 2 | 3 | 4 | 5 | 6 | 7 | ■ | 8 | 9 | 10 | 11 | 12 | 13 | ■ | 14 | 15 | ■ | 16 | 17 | 18 | 19 |
|---|---|---|---|---|---|---|---|---|---|----|----|----|----|---|----|----|---|----|----|----|----|
|   |   |   |   |   |   |   |   |   |   |    |    |    |    |   |    |    |   |    |    |    |    |

| | | |
|---|---|---|
| 1. T Ì ___ N U | (_____ – ____) | "   " |
| 2. H ____ | (_____) | "   " |
| 3. ___ U L | (_____) | "   " |
| 4. M ____ | (_____) | "   " |
| 5. S E ___ | (____) | "   " |
| 6. O ___ | (__) | "   " |
| 7. F R A ___ O | (_____) | "   " |
| 8. ___ T I A | (_____) | "   " |
| 9. H A PX ___ | (_____) | "   " |
| 10. W U ___ O | (_____) | "   " |
| 11. Y AW N ___ | (_____) | "   " |
| 12. M U ___ E | (_____) | "   " |
| 13. N A ___ R | (_____) | "   " |
| 14. O ___ O ' | (_____) | "   " |
| 15. O M ___ M | (_____) | "   " |
| 16. S ____ AW N G | (_____) | "   " |
| 17. S R ___ K | (_____) | "   " |
| 18. O ___ T U | (_____) | "   " |
| 19. K A L TX ___ | (_____) | "   " |

## Puzzle 14 — Tìkawng txan — RDA Management training material

Na'vi phrase: " _____ ?"

| 1 | 2 | 3 | 4 | 5 | ■ | 6 | 7 | 8 | ■ | 9 | 10 | 11 | ■ | 12 | 13 | 14 |

| | | |
|---|---|---|
| 1. ___ U | _____ | " " |
| 2. S ___ U L A NG | _____ | " " |
| 3. NG ___ | _____ | " " |
| 4. M EY ___ | _____ | " " |
| 5. TS KX ___ | _____ | " " |
| 6. P E ___ Y A | _____ | " " |
| 7. EY ___ | _____ | " " |
| 8. S ___ M | _____ | " " |
| 9. H A ___ EY | _____ | " " |
| 10. TS ___ O KX | _____ | " " |
| 11. T _____ NG | _____ | " " |
| 12. NG AW _____ | _____ | " " |
| 13. E ___ N | _____ | " " |
| 14. K A ___ | _____ | " " |

## Puzzle 15 — Tìkawng nìtxan — RDA Executive training material

Na'vi phrase: " _____ ?"

| 1 | 2 | 3 | 4 | ■ | 5 | 6 | ■ | 7 | 8 | 9 | 10 | ■ | 11 | 12 | 13 | 14 |

| | | |
|---|---|---|
| 1. T Ì ___ | _____ | " " |
| 2. T EY ___ | _____ | " " |
| 3. S ___ EW | _____ | " " |
| 4. Y ___ R | _____ | " " |
| 5. ' AW ___ O | _____ | " " |
| 6. ' ___ P E | _____ | " " |
| 7. ___ Ì T RR | _____ | " " |
| 8. L U M ___ E | _____ | " " |
| 9. I R AY ___ | _____ | " " |
| 10. ___ Ì N | _____ | " " |
| 11. ___ E T | _____ | " " |
| 12. ___ Ì K | _____ | " " |
| 13. TX ___ N | _____ | " " |
| 14. ___ Ì M | _____ | " " |

# Reverse Na'vi Crossword

This was supposed to be an easy puzzle; something to relax and play with at your leisure. We made a crossword and filled in all of the answers for you. All you had to do was to cross out each word in the puzzle and write in the English meaning *(word or word approximation)* below the puzzle. Well those *jerks* in accounting are at it again!* They have (once again . . .) thought it was funny to paste little white dots all over the puzzle, obscuring many of the letters. <u>So now you get to</u> figure out the missing letters *and then* cross out each word in the puzzle and write in the English meaning on the lines below the puzzle.

Good luck!

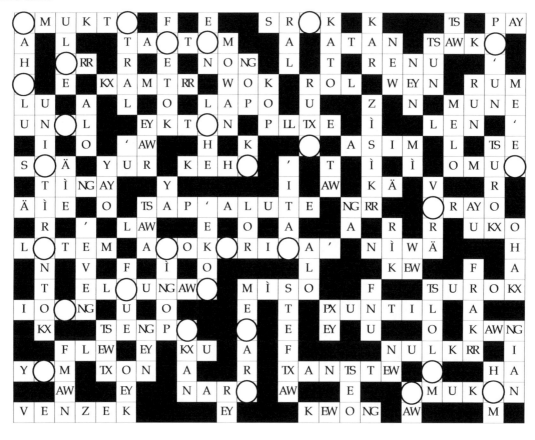

* See Final Exam in *Learn Na'vi the Easy Way!*

# 3-Letter Word Puzzle

In this puzzle we have gone ahead and filled in all of the Na'vi words for you. But in the process we alphabetized the clues, so you will have to match up each clue with each answer in the puzzle. Below the puzzle we have provided you some space to work out your answers and to write in each clue word (*nì'Ìnglìsì*) as it matches up to each answer (*nì'Na'vi*).

| ACROSS |
|---|
| Ball |
| Blue |
| Calm |
| Chase |
| Choose |
| Dance |
| Drink |
| Great or noble |
| Mighty |
| Sing |
| Suggest |
| Tomorrow |
| Turn (instance) |

| DOWN |
|---|
| Approach |
| Beautiful |
| Cause |
| Correct |
| Dry |
| Full |
| Look at |
| Mountain |
| Quiet (be quiet) |
| They |
| Thing (action), deed |
| Try |
| Yellow |

*P r a c t i c e      a r e a*

| ACROSS | |
|---|---|
| *nì'Ìnglìsì:* | *nì'Na'vi:* |
| | |
| | |
| | |
| | |
| | |
| | |
| | |
| | |
| | |
| | |
| | |

| DOWN | |
|---|---|
| *nì'Ìnglìsì:* | *nì'Na'vi:* |
| | |
| | |
| | |
| | |
| | |
| | |
| | |
| | |
| | |
| | |
| | |

# Na'vi Mini-Word Searches

We have added a slight twist to these words. We have given you a word bank in English. All of the words in this puzzles should be relatively easy to remember so go ahead and test your skill. We think you will get most of the words without having to look in the back of the book. *Words read left to right, top to bottom, and diagonally (top to bottom/left to right).*

```
K   E   H   E   H   V   E   N   U   W   M  AW  EY
A   H   A   H   A   S   E   Y   A   T  EY   A   K
L   U   Ì   N   H   Ì   W   Y   U   R   P   M   K
TX  L   W   '  AW   L   O   F   H   K   I   N   Ä
Ì   T   H   I   I   W   F   T   I   A   M   Ä  TS
M   E   A   T   A   N   V   A   W   R  PX   K   E
E   R   S   E   L   T   U  NG  PX  U   N   Ì   O
N   U   M   E   R   O   L   P  AW   M   A   T   S
A  TX   '   I   T   A   N   M   U  NG  E   Ì   R
R   E   I   R  AY   O   P  LL  TX   E   R   K   A
I   N   I   Ä   Y   O   M   T   I  NG  AY AW   N
S   R  NG   K   E   R   E   '   O   M  NG   E
```

## WORD LIST:

AGREE _____

AND (1) _____

AND (2) _____

ARM _____

ART _____

ASK _____

BLUE _____

BRAIN _____

BRANCH _____

CALM _____

DAUGHTER _____

DONE _____

DRINK (NOUN) _____

DRINK (VERB) _____

EAT _____

EVIL _____

EYE _____

EYES _____

FOOT _____

FULL _____

GO _____

GRAB _____

HEAD _____

HELLO _____

HELP _____

LEAD _____

LEARN _____

LIGHT _____

LITTLE _____

NO _____

NOT _____

NOW _____

ONCE _____

PLEASE _____

PREVIOUS _____

SEVEN _____

SING _____

SLEEP _____

SON _____

SPEAK _____

STUDY _____

TAKE _____

TEACH _____

THANKS _____

TRUTH _____

WASH _____

WEAK _____

WORM _____

YES _____

```
'  A  M  P  I  I  K  A  R  Y  U  F  K  A  M  E  F
EY K  T  A  N  O  NG O  Ì  S  E  T  A  W  Y  U  R
L  M  U  N  E  A  A  E  K  NG AY Ä  O  N  T  U  A
A  F  T  I  A  NG T  A  R  O  N  R  P  U  K  A  P
N  S  O  M  S  K  I  E  N  E  Y  TS M  U  K  E  O
H  U  F  W  E  R  Z  Ì  S  Ì  T  Y  O  M  V  T  M
K  TS TX T  M  V  A  S  Y  U  L  A  NG Y  O  O  K
E  M  O  U  P  RR M  N  TS E  '  A  K  RR L  M  E
L  U  N  NG U  T  I  K  E  L  U  T  R  A  L  P  M
K  K  E  M  L  E  K  I  E  Y  P  Ì  W  O  PX A  P
U  A  S  R  EW P  Y  N  KX H  E  Y  AY O  K  EW E
Y  N  T  Ì  NG Y  U  A  A  Y  E  L  T  U  S  I  K
E  M  A  K  T  O  N  M  K  Ì  Y  E  V  A  M  E  AW
P  A  L  U  L  U  K  A  N  V  E  N  Z  E  K  V  NG
Z  E  K  W  Ä  M  E  S  A  '  N  O  K  S  KX AW NG
F  Y  A  P  E  PX U  N  T  I  L  Y  F  Ì  F  Y  A
```

## WORD LIST:

| | | | |
|---|---|---|---|
| ALLOW | _____ | MOUTH | _____ |
| ANIMAL | _____ | NIGHT | _____ |
| BAD | _____ | NO | _____ |
| BIRD | _____ | NOSE | _____ |
| BROTHER | _____ | PAY ATTENTION! | _____ |
| CHIEF OR LEADER | _____ | RAIN | _____ |
| CLOUD | _____ | RIDE | _____ |
| DANCE | _____ | RIGHT (direction) | _____ |
| DEMON | _____ | SEE (physically) | _____ |
| EAR | _____ | SEE (spiritually) | _____ |
| EAT | _____ | SISTER | _____ |
| EIGHT | _____ | SIX | _____ |
| ELBOW | _____ | SKY | _____ |
| EVERYONE | _____ | STUDY | _____ |
| FATHER | _____ | TEACHER | _____ |
| FINGER | _____ | THANATOR | _____ |
| FLOWER | _____ | THIS WAY | _____ |
| FRIEND | _____ | TIME | _____ |
| GIVE | _____ | TOE | _____ |
| GOODBYE | _____ | TOUCH | _____ |
| HOME | _____ | TRUE | _____ |
| HOMETREE | _____ | TWO | _____ |
| HOT | _____ | WASH | _____ |
| HOW | _____ | WHAT (action) | _____ |
| HUNT | _____ | WHAT (thing) | _____ |
| LEAF | _____ | WIND | _____ |
| LEFT (direction) | _____ | YEAR | _____ |
| LEG | _____ | YES | _____ |
| ME | _____ | YOU | _____ |
| MORON | _____ | ZERO | _____ |
| MOTHER | _____ | | |

# Na'vi word substitution (slightly advanced)

In this exercise we have secretly replaced common English words with their Na'vi equivalent. As the stories and rhymes are in English, with Na'vi word substitutions, we will be following English grammar rules, so we are using the Na'vi root words. Simply replace the Na'vi word below with the English equivalent word. Try not o look it up in the dictionary. If you take a moment to look at the sentence, you should be able to figure out most the words easily. (But just in case, we put the original translation at the end).

### Example: "Hey Diddle Diddle" nursery rhyme

Hey diddle diddle, the cat **sì** the fiddle,

_____ (write in "and")

The cow **spolä** over the moon.  *(sp<ol>ä = spä + <ol> or "past tense" = jumped)*

_____ (write in jumped)

The little dog laughed to **tse'a** such **fun** —

(write in "see") _____ _____ (write in "tì'o'")

and the dish **tolul    neto** with the spoon.  *(t<ol>ul= tul + <ol> or "past tense of run" = ran)*

_____ _____ (write in "ran" and "away")

### Okay, now we do it without hint words. Good luck!

One of the most famous speeches in history: (original speech appears below if you need the words)

**PLEASE NOTE:** *The exact words may require heavy grammatical changes which you have not learned in this book, and are far too omplicated for "just starting out" so basic words appear to help you through* simple word substitution. *If the entire speech were to be actually translated into Na'vi it would appear entirely different. That level of understanding Na'vi is far beyond "starting out," or "beginner."*

**Tsìng** score **sì   kinä   ayzìsìt** ago **ayoeng** forefathers **zolamunge** forth on this continent a **mip** nation,

___ ___ ___ ___ _____ _____

conceived **mì** Liberty, **ulte** dedicated to the proposition that **nìwotx aytutan** are **ngolop teng.**

___ ___ ___ ___ _____ _____.

Now **ayoeng** are engaged **mì** a great civil **tsam,** testing whether that nation, **fu** any nation, so

___ ___ _____, ___

conceived **sì** so dedicated, **tsun** long endure. **Ayoeng** are met on a **txan** battle-field of **tsa'u tsam.**

___ ___ ___ ___ ___ ___.

**Ayoeng** have **za'u** to dedicate a **hapxì** of **tsa'u** field, as a final resting place for those **tupe fìtsenge**

___ _____ ___ ___ ___ _____

**tolìng** their lives that that nation might **rey.**

___ _____.

52

It **lu** altogether fitting **sì** proper that **ayoeng** should do **fìkem**.

Slä, in a larger sense, **ayoeng tsun ke** dedicate . . . **ayoeng tsun ke** consecrate . . .

**ayoeng tsun ke** hallow **fìtseng** ground. The **tstew aysmukan**, living **sì kerusey**,

**tupe** struggled **fìtsenge**, have consecrated it, far above our poor power to **sung** or detract.

The world will **hìm** note, nor long remember **'upe ayoeng** say **fìtsenge**, **slä** it can **kawkrr** forget

**kempe** they did **fìtsenge**. It is for us the **rerey**, rather, to be dedicated **fìtseng**

to the unfinished work **a    ayfo    tupe** fought **fìtseng** have thus far so nobly advanced.

It **lu** rather for us to be here dedicated to the **txan** task remaining **eo** us—

that **ta** these honored dead **ayoeng munge** increased devotion to that cause

for **a ayfo** gave the last full measure of devotion—that we here highly resolve that these

dead shall **ke** have died **mì** vain—that **fì'u** nation, under God, shall have a new birth of

freedom—**ulte** that government of **Na'vi**, by **Na'vi**, for **Na'vi**,

shall **ke** perish **ta** the earth.

*In his own words:*

Four score and seven years ago our fathers brought forth on this continent a new nation, conceived in Liberty, and dedicated to the proposition that "all men are created equal."

Now we are engaged in a great civil war, testing whether that nation, or any nation, so conceived and so dedicated, can long endure. We are met on a great battle-field of that war. We have come to dedicate a portion of that field, as a final resting place for those who here gave their lives that that nation might live. It is altogether fitting and proper that we should do this.

But, in a larger sense, we can not dedicate . . . we can not consecrate . . . we can not hallow this ground. The brave men, living and dead, who struggled here, have consecrated it, far above our poor power to add or detract. The world will little note, nor long remember what we say here, but it can never forget what they did here. It is for us the living, rather, to be dedicated here to the unfinished work which they who fought here have thus far so nobly advanced. It is rather for us to be here dedicated to the great task remaining before us—that from these honored dead we take increased devotion to that cause for which they gave the last full measure of devotion—that we here highly resolve that these dead shall not have died in vain—that this nation, under God, shall have a new birth of freedom—and that government of the people, by the people, for the people, shall not perish from the earth.

# Fun Na'vi songs!

I got the idea to write fun parodies of classic children's songs shortly after seeing *Avatar*. My line of reasoning was that the psychological trauma suffered by the Na'vi children would find itself expressed in humor and song, as children are ever-resilient and the Na'vi kids were, after all, indoctrinated in earth-based education systems. I figured the result would be a hybrid of human and Na'vi concepts expressed in a mish-mash of human and Na'vi language. But what made the whole of it workable was that it was just fun to make fun of sawtute. You may have heard us sing a few of these songs on the *Radio Avatar* podcast. Here are the lyrics. You might want to write your own songs. It's a great way to have fun expressing yourself nì'Na'vi (*"in Na'vi"*).

One word of warning though: The grammar used in these example songs is atrocious and should not be taken as correct phraseology. These songs were written within a month of the movie coming out, back when we had a handful of words to play with and very little understanding of the workings of the Na'vi language. Add to that the fact that the few words we did have were strung together to best match the tempo of the earth-song melody and create a humorous poke at humans. Songwriters are notorious for bending the rules of grammar to create a good hook or memorable lyric.

*One easy way to help learn common words and phrases in a new language is to sing short, fun songs that get stuck in your head.* This is one of the ways children learn grammar and vocabulary all over the world. <u>Once they learn a song they like it stays with them for the rest of their life.</u> So in that vein, I have composed a few songs to help get your started. I hope these will create an interest in you to write better songs. Take any melody you know and simply replace the words to your liking. With just a little practice you might become the Na'vi "Weird Al Yankovic."

This first one you may not know by name, but the melody is simple and familiar. In this case, please imagine Na'vi children making up a song about the bad sky-people. The horror they endured, especially in the Omticaya clan (death of Hometree and the Tree of Voices), but also any clan whose mommies and daddies had to fight (and most die) fighting the sky-people does not easily go away. <u>So you make fun of it</u> *(see: "Ring Around the Rosy")*. This is the basis for many of the old children's songs throughout history, where children would sing about death and the plague. So, without further adieu, here is the first installment: The "I hate Bosco" song. (I will try to remember to post the original OTR commercial on the *Radio Avatar* podcast)

*A long, long time ago, there were popular children's songs. This was one of them:*

| **I hate Bosco song** | **Fun (Post-Avatar) Na'vi children's song!** | |
|---|---|---|
| | *(sing along!)* | |
| *I hate Bosco* | | |
| *It's not the drink for me* | *Oe Tawtute!* | (I Tawtute!) |
| *(alternatively: It's full of TNT [or DDT])* | *Oel plltxe 'inglìsì* | (I speak English) |
| *My mommy put it in my milk* | *Oel tamswon ftu alìm* | (I fly from far away) |
| *To try to poison me* | *ulte Oel skola'a ayutral!* | (and I [chop down*] lots of trees!) |
| *One day I fooled Mommy* | *Oe lu vrrtep* | (I'm a demon) |
| *I slipped some in her tea* | *Oel tamspang oeyä sa'nu* | (I killed my own mommy!) |
| *And now I have no mommy* | *Ha set Oel kerelku si Eywa'eveng* | (So now I live on Pandora) |
| *To try to poison me!* | *ulte Oel 'eko Na'vi!* | (And I attack Na'vi!) |

*Unfinished ditty to the tune of Mary Had a Little Lamb:*

*Mary yimom eltungawng,*
*eltungawng,*
*eltungawng,*
*Mary yimom eltungawng,*
*and she wen't insane!*

Basically: Mary *(generic tawtute skxawng)* ate a brainworm (x3, and repeat) and she went insane.

❖   ❖   ❖

***Row Row Row Your Boat*** appeared on the podcast as well:

*Row, Row, Row Your Boat* song
(Oldest known version: The earliest printing of the song is from 1852.)
Na'vi edition by *Kaltxì Palulukan.*

| *nìNa'vi (in Na'vi)* | *nìInglìsì (in English)* |
|---|---|
| *'Upe, 'upe, upe lu ral* | What, what, what's (the) meaning |
| *\*Tawvrrtep – yä ìnlglìsì?* | of sky-demon words? |
| *Kawtu omum, kawtu omum* | No one knows, no one knows |
| *Sawtute lu askxawng* | Sky people are blind ("un-seeing" morons) |

*\*This is a totally made-up word used to make the song funnier. It is tongue-in-cheek and not meant to be taken as canon. Additionally, I offer no guarantees on grammatical correctness, as there is – at this printing – only one Tawtute alive who can tell us exactly what is and what is not "Na'vi correctus summae."*

❖   ❖   ❖

***Old Mc Donald*** was actually the very first song to be flayed alive by my nefarious machinations. I had learned Na'vi through visual text (not spoken word) and I developed the bad habit of pronouncing *irayo* "eye-RAY-oh" instead of "ee-rye-oh." I finally corrected this by walking around saying "ee-rye-oh" over and over and it hit me how much that sounded like *"ee-eye-ee-eye-oh."* Thus was born the mad dash to convert all songs into Na'vi, or Na'vi parodies of the English versions.

Na'vi *Old Mc Donald* song.
(Oldest known version: *The Kingdom of the Birds,* published in 1719-1720.)
Na'vi edition by *Kaltxì Palulukan* with a <u>generous grammatical correction</u> and overall "tightening up" by *Prrton.*

| *nìNa'vi (in Na'vi)* | *nìInglìsì (in English)* |
|---|---|
| *Olo'eyktanta tukrut-timel* | I just got a spear from the Chief of our clan |
| *Iray–Iray–oooo* | Thank you. Thank you. (Soooo.) |
| *Ha oeyä tukrufa tskxekeng óe* | So I practice with my spear wherever I go |
| *Iray–Iray–oooo* | Thank you. Thank you. (Soooo.) |
| *Set takuk mìfitseng* | Now I strike over here, |
| *Ult' 'eko mìsatseng* | And attack over there. |
| *fitseng takuk, tsatseng 'eko* | Here a strike, there attack! |
| *Takuk takuk! Makto KO!* | We're off to ride, so watch your back! |
| *Olo'eyktanta tukrut-timel* | I received a spear from the Chief of our clan |
| *Iray–Iray–oooo* | Thank you. Thank you. (Soooo.) |

NOTE: This song, in it's current form, is almost impossible to sing. We did a savagely butchered version on *Radio Avatar* at the end of one episode. We got through *"olo'eyktan timing oeri tukru–iray, iray-ooo."*

Okay, so notes: The point of these songs is to illustrate how easily words and phrases can be taken from Na'vi and applied to universally -known melodies—even with the severely limited number of words we now possess. We don't need more <u>words</u>. ***We need more creativity!*** This is just another way of learning and memorizing Na'vi words and phrases. I do not mean to imply that friendly little Na'vi *ayevi* sit around making fun of their (previous) Tawvrrtep colonialist oppressors—but that is admittedly where the idea for "Na'vi children songs" *(ayway 'evengru Na'vi?)* originated.

**IF YOU HAVE AN IDEA FOR A SONG,** by all means write it. <u>Write it</u>, <u>sing it</u>, <u>record it</u>, <u>give it away</u>. Sing it at parties, sing it at conventions. Help others learn this beautiful language by sharing your passion and creativity. Get ready for *A2* by knowing your Na'vi. If these rather banal examples have inspired you to create something better, something to share with the world, then my job is done here.

Just because we may never get around to actually recording the following songs I am including the lyrics here. These are popular songs from various artists and genres, and they are not specifically *ni'Na'vi* but designed to entertain the average *Avatar* fan. If you have a band and you would like to have fun singing songs about *Avatar* perhaps you might get some ideas from these parodies:

Queen's **We Will Rock You** re-envisioned by *KP!* (me). If you heard Tìng's "Culture Corner" from *episode one* you will catch the "big man" reference. This would make a fun sing-along at Comicon.

*Buddy, you're a boy*
*makin' big noise*
*playing in the trees*
*gonna be a big man some day*
*You go mud on your face*
*animal grace*
*flying your banshee all over the place\**

*singin:*
*Toooh-ruk Toooh-ruk MAKTO!*
*Toooh-ruk Toooh-ruk MAKTO!*

*Buddy you're a young man*
*taronyu*
*tsamsiyu warrior\*\**
*gonna take on the R--D--A*

*War paint on your face*
*leadin' the chase*
*wavin' your spear all in my face*

*Singin:*
*Toooh-ruk Toooh-ruk MAKTO!*
*Toooh-ruk Toooh-ruk MAKTO!*

*Olo'eyktan you're a big man*
*elder member of the clan\*\**
*helped us to win--the--day*

*You got lines on your face*
*Earned your place*
*Savin' our planet from the human RACE!*

*Toooh-ruk Toooh-ruk MAKTO!*
*Toooh-ruk Toooh-ruk MAKTO!*

\* From the *A.S.G.* <u>Every</u> Na'vi *'evi* has a toy banshee.
\*\* These lines are very difficult but are no different than many songs that require skill to vocalize.

## The *Avatarization* of Don McLean's ***American Pie*** by *Kaltxì Palulukan!* and *Alton Dean*

*A long long time ago*
*I can still remember how the Na'vi children used to smile*
*And I was part of the mission If we could make the people listen*
*Then, maybe there would be peace for a while But sawtute made me shiver*
*Only pain could we deliver Death rained from the kunsip I couldn't take one more step*

*I can't remember if I cried*
*When I saw the tree lain on it's side*
*But something touched me deep inside*
*The day Kelutral died*

*So Bye-bye, Pandoran Life*
*Tried to make a difference, but I wasted my time*
*The man is out to get me and there's nowhere to hide*
*This'll be the day that I die*
*This'll be the day that I die*

*Did you come here from above*
*And do you have faith in Eywa's love If the Tsahik tells you so*
*Oh, do you believe in miracles*
*Can Pandora save us from ourselves*
*And can you help me to believe again*
*Well, I know we came for a prize*
*'Cause I saw it with my own two eyes*
*Two world's slashed and burned*
*Oh, nothing have we learned*

*I was an apprentice driver – (the) last in line*
*Just waiting for my chance to shine*
*But I knew I was out of time*
*The day Kelutral died*
*I started singing bye-bye, Pandoran Life*
*Tried to make a difference*
*but I wasted my time*
*The man is out to get me and there's nowhere to hide*
*(singin') This'll be the day that I die*
*This'll be the day that I die*

*Now for six years we'd been on our own*
*Selfridge had agreed to leave us alone*
*At least that's how it used to be*
*When Jake spoke to Mo'at and Eytukan*
*In an avatar borrowed from---ma smuktan*
*In a voice that begged sanity-ee*

*Oh, and while Eytukan was looking down*
*The colonel came and shot him down*
*Killed by the sacred tree*
*Oh how I wish it was me*
*And while the Colonel hit his mark*
*Selfridge joked with snide remark*
*And we sang dirges in the dark*
*The day the kelutral died*

*We were singin'*
*Bye-bye, Pandoran Life*
*Tried to make a difference, but I wasted my time*
*The man is out to get me and there's nowhere to hide*
*This'll be the day that I die*
*This'll be the day that I die*

*Helter Skelter all over again*
*The birds flew off with an evil plan*
*Five clicks out, and closing fast*
*The shuttle crashed foul on the grass*
*But the Colonel tried with one last pass*
*With the boss on the sidelines, in a cast*

*Now the half-time air was sweet perfume*
*While the Sergeants played a marching tune*
*We all got up to dance*
*Oh, but we never got the chance*

*'Cause sawtute tried to take the field*
*Eywa's band refused to yield*
*Do you recall what was revealed*
*The day the Kelutral died*

*We started singin'*
*Bye-bye, Pandoran Life*
*Tried to make a difference,*
*but I wasted my time*
*The man is out to get me and there's nowhere to hide*
*This'll be the day that I die*
*This'll be the day that I die*

*Oh, and there we were all in one place*
*A generation lost in space*
*With no time left to start again*
*So come on, Jakesooly – Jake be quick*
*The devil's lit a dynamite stick*
*'Cause fire is the Colonel's only friend*

*Oh, and as I watched him on his stage*
*My hands were clenched in fists of rage*
*No demon spawned from hell*
*Could match that iron will*
*And as the flames climbed high into the night*
*To light the sacrificial rite*
*I saw the colonel laughing with delight*
*The day Kelutral died*

*He was singin'*
*Bye-bye, Pandoran Life*
*Tried to make a difference, but I wasted my time*
*Valhalla's calling to me and it's time to decide*
*Whether this'll be the day that I die*
*This'll be the day that I die*

*I met a girl whose skin was blue*
*And I asked her for some happy news*
*But she just screamed and turned away*
*I went down to the sacred grove*
*Where I'd heard the voices just days before*
*But the 'dozers had pushed the trees away*
*And in the trees the children screamed*
*The lovers cried, and the walkers dreamed*
*But not a word was spoken*
*The church bells all were broken*

*And the men who caused all this mirth*
*Just to increase their corporate worth*
*They caught the last plane back to Earth*
*The day Kelutral died*

*They were singin'*
*Bye-bye, Pandoran Life*
*Tried to make a difference*
*but I wasted my time*
*Eywa's out to get me and there's nowhere to hide*
*This'll be the day that I die*
*This'll be the day that I die*

Currently I am working on a rendition of Frank Zappa's *Valley Girl* ("*She's a Na'vi Girl*") and Norm Greenbaum's *Spirit in the Sky* (soon to be *Spirit in the Tree*). **If you have a band** and you want to sing these songs just email me and I will send you the lyrics.

<u>*Na'vi Girl*</u> excerpt

*Na'vi girl*
*She's a Na'vi girl*
*Na'vi girl*
*She's a Na'vi girl*
*Okay sìltsan*
*Fer sure, fer sure*
*She's a Na'vi girl*
*In a Na'vi world*
*Okay sìltsan*
*Fer sure, fer sure*
*She's a —*

**Like, oh my Eywa!**
*(Na'vi girl)*
**Like – nìwotx!**
*(Na'vi girl)*
**Hometree is just like so bitchen!**
*(Na'vi girl)*
**There's like a Starbucks,**
*(Na'vi girl)*
**and really cool txon tìrey**
*I love going into like the loom and stuff*
*I like buy the neatest mini-skirts and stuff—*
*Its like so bitchen cuz like everybodys like*
*Super-super nice... Its like so bitchen...*

*On Kelutral, there she goes*
*She just bought some bitchen clothes*
*Tosses her head n flips her hair*
*She got a whole bunch of nothin in there*

**So this Tawtute walks up to me and asks**
*Do you wanna Srew srak?*
*And I was totally like:*
*What are you, some kind of skxawng srak?*
*Look vrrtep—take a good look at oeru*
*and then look at ngaru.*
*I mean, as if!*
*What a ngawng!*
*I'm sure!*

<u>*Spirt in the Tree*</u> excerpt

(as you can see it needs a little more work)

*When I die and they lay me to rest*
*Gonna go to the tree that's the best*
*When it's time for me to leave*
*Goin' up to the spirit in the tree*
*Goin' up to the spirit in the tree*
*That's where I'm gonna go when I leave*
*When I die and they lay me to rest*
*Gonna go to the tree that's the best*

*Prepare yourself you know it's a must*
*Gotta have a friend in Eywa*
*So you know that when you leave*
*She's gonna recommend you*
*To the spirit in the tree*
*Gonna recommend you*
*To the spirit in the tree*
*That's where you're gonna go when you leave*
*When you die and they lay you to rest*
*You're gonna go to the tree that's the best*

*Never been a sinner I never sinned*
*I got a friend in Eywa*
*So you know that when I die*
*She's gonna set me up with*
*The spirit in the tree*
*Oh set me up with the spirit in the tree*
*That's where I'm gonna go when I leave*
*When I die and they lay me to rest*
*I'm gonna go to the tree that's the best*
*Go to the tree that's the best*

So there you have it. There are <u>no sacred cows</u>. Have fun expressing yourself through music *sì* Na'vi. When you are inspired just start writing out ideas and change words until they fit your melody. Over time you will become more proficient—but start here. Start now, an make the world around you more fun.

# SOLUTIONS

## Quotation Puzzle Fun

Puzzle #1: *Oeri ta peyä fahew akewong ontu teya längu.*

Puzzle #2: *Fayvrrtep fitsenge lu kxanì*

Puzzle #3: *Sìfmetokit emzola'u ohel. Ätxäle si tsnì livu oheru Uniltaron.*

Puzzle #4: *Ma Eytukan, lu oeru aylì'u frapor. Aylì'u na ayskxe mì te'lan.*

Puzzle #5: *Eo ayoeng lu txana tìkawng. Sawtute zera'u fte fol Kelutralti skiva'a. Pìyähem fitseng ye'rìn.*

Puzzle #6: *Oel ngati kameie, ma Tsmukan, ulte ngaru seiyi irayo. Ngari hu Eywa salew tirea, tokx 'ì'awn slu Na'viyä hapxì.*

---

## Daily actions and interactions

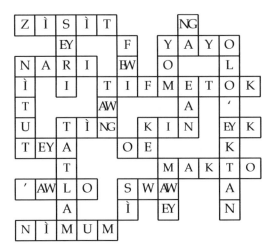

## Na'vi Letter Block

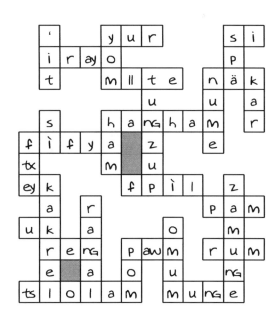

# Na'vi sudoku

## Puzzle 1:

| mune | volaw | pxey | kinä | 'aw | mrr | pukap | vol | tsìng |
|------|-------|------|------|-----|-----|-------|-----|-------|
| pukap | tsìng | kinä | pxey | vol | volaw | 'aw | mrr | mune |
| 'aw | vol | mrr | mune | tsìng | pukap | kinä | volaw | pxey |
| volaw | kinä | vol | 'aw | mrr | mune | pxey | tsìng | pukap |
| mrr | pxey | mune | tsìng | pukap | kinä | volaw | 'aw | vol |
| tsìng | 'aw | pukap | vol | volaw | pxey | mune | kinä | mrr |
| vol | mune | tsìng | volaw | pxey | 'aw | mrr | pukap | kinä |
| pxey | mrr | volaw | pukap | kinä | tsìng | vol | mune | 'aw |
| kinä | pukap | 'aw | mrr | mune | vol | tsìng | pxey | volaw |

## Puzzle 2:

| kinä | pxey | mune | vol | 'aw | tsìng | mrr | pukap | volaw |
|------|------|------|-----|-----|-------|-----|-------|-------|
| pukap | vol | mrr | volaw | kinä | pxey | tsìng | 'aw | mune |
| volaw | 'aw | tsìng | mune | pukap | mrr | kinä | pxey | vol |
| mrr | pukap | vol | tsìng | mune | kinä | pxey | volaw | 'aw |
| mune | kinä | pxey | 'aw | vol | volaw | pukap | tsìng | mrr |
| tsìng | volaw | 'aw | pxey | mrr | pukap | mune | vol | kinä |
| 'aw | tsìng | volaw | kinä | pxey | mune | vol | mrr | pukap |
| vol | mrr | kinä | pukap | tsìng | 'aw | volaw | mune | pxey |
| pxey | mune | pukap | mrr | volaw | vol | 'aw | kinä | tsìng |

# Na'vi language learning resources, *Avatar* fan sites and creations

## If we have missed <u>your</u> favorite website or Na'vi/*Avatar* resource please email me immediately at *corrections@radioavatar.com*.

Please note that many of these projects have been or will be abandoned by their creators over time. All are listed here in the hopes they will be revived or archived. Quality of each project <u>varies</u>. This is just a comprehensive list of known fan creations and official FOX/James Cameron's *Avatar*™ resources.

## Major *Avatar* fan sites, groups, and podcasts:

**Forums:**
*Avatar* Forums: http://avatarthemovieforum.com
*Avatar* Movie Club: http://www.avatarmovieclub.com/
*Avatar* Movie Fansite: http://www.avatar-movie.org/
*Avatar* Movie Forums: http://www.avatar-forums.com
*Avatar* Prime Forums: http://avatarprime.net/
LearnNa'vi.org: http://www.learnnavi.org
Na'vi Blue *Avatar* movie forums: http://www.naviblue.com

**Podcasts:**
Na'vi Lessons podcast: http://navilessons.podomatic.com/
Prrton's podcast: http://upxare.podomatic.com/
**Radio Avatar** fan podcast: http://www.RadioAvatar.com **(*The world's largest Avatar fan creation!*)**
It's like a podcast version of *Saturday Night Live* meets *60 Minutes* but we are all broke amateurs.

**Facebook:**
http://www.facebook.com/RadioAvatar
There are so many *Avatar* fan groups and individuals on FB that you just have to see it for yourself. It is hard to know which account is the official one.

**Twitter:**
http://twitter.com/officialavatar    This purports to be the "offical" *Avatar* movie account.
*Tweet them and TELL THEM you want better language learning materials!!*

## Na'vi language learning resources:

Most everything can be found at learnnavi.org (above) but here are some direct links:
**Eight's Na'vi Rhyming dictionary:** In a word—*AWESOME!!*
http://www.scribd.com/doc/25465697/The-Sub-Na%E2%80%99vi-Rhyming-Dictionary

**Tree of Voices (Na'vi "Rosetta Stone" clone)**
http://treeofvoices.dyndns.org/

**List of current resources:**
http://wiki.learnnavi.org/index.php/Resources

# Avatar comics (spoofs) online:

These are *really fun.* most of them are downright hilarious — all are fan creations.

**The infamous Avatard comics from Rooster Teeth:**
http://images.roosterteeth.com/assets/media/9_4b3147278edda.jpg
http://images.roosterteeth.com/assets/media/9_4b4fa410d6060.jpg
http://images.roosterteeth.com/assets/media/9_4b52723dcf6c6.jpg
http://images.roosterteeth.com/assets/media/9_4b56119a33124.jpg
http://images.roosterteeth.com/assets/media/9_4b58df3bbc5f1.jpg

**Foxtrot daily comic takes on Avatar"**
http://www.foxtrot.com/comics/2010-02-21-cefc12e3.gif

**A "3-D" attempt at online Avatar comic**
http://www.actiongravy.com/images/avatarice3D.gif

**Just another "Deviant Art Genius" (fan)**
http://fc05.deviantart.net/fs70/i/2010/003/3/d/Avatar_Na__vi_Meme___Mine_by_Manisoke.jpg

**Just another "Deviant Art Genius" (fan) #2  \*\*\****Carmen Sipes weighs in*\*\*\*
http://fc09.deviantart.net/fs70/f/2010/043/0/7/Navi_Meme_Fun_by_Thatseattlegirl.jpg

**"i can haz"** *Avatar* **movie in 5 panels (do not view if you have NOT seen** *Avatar* **yet)**
http://s.buzzfed.com/static/imagebuzz/terminal01/2009/12/21/14/i-can-has-avatar-spoilers-2086-1261422208-12.jpg

**okay, this one is just "wrong" (but it has the Colnel!! and an** *Airplane* **reference)**
http://fc00.deviantart.net/fs71/f/2010/001/4/1/THE_LAST_AIRBENDER_by_ConcentrationMoon.jpg

**And this is my response to the above comic — or "my impression of Salvador Dali**
http://www.dustywhite.net/Navi/MINI.gif

**Carmen Sipes gives us yet a NEW character**
http://fc07.deviantart.net/fs71/f/2010/068/8/3/Hiirawr_page_1_by_Thatseattlegirl.jpg
http://fc07.deviantart.net/fs71/f/2010/068/8/3/Hiirawr_page_1_by_Thatseattlegirl.jpg
http://fc04.deviantart.net/fs71/f/2010/068/d/5/Little_Rawr_Page_2_by_Thatseattlegirl.jpg
*(Seriously: this girl is a cartoon machine)*

**Avatar spoof comic:**
http://fc09.deviantart.net/fs70/f/2010/025/1/7/Avatarded_The_Turd_by_IZRA.jpg

**And this may be the BEST AVATAR COMIC —** *EVER!!*
http://loyalkng.com/wp-content/uploads/2010/01/avatard-random-domain-james-cameron-israel-espinoza-avatar-cats-yarn-ball.jpg

**\*\*\* Official Avatar movie sites \*\*\***
Official Movie site: http://www.avatarmovie.com/
Official Movie site (Spain) http://www.avatarpelicula.es/ *(very cool)*
The Pandorapedia http://www.pandorapedia.com/

**Greatest director in the history of everything**
IMDb: http://www.imdb.com/name/nm0000116/

*The following people made this book possible:*

# CONTRIBUTORS

**Ilonka Papp** — *(Girl on the font cover of this book)*
Ilonka is an artist and model who currently lives in Pureto Rico. Her dream is to be able to afford to come to the United States and study professional movie make-up in Los Angeles. She fell in love with *Avatar* and spent several weeks creating and perfecting her make-up and costume on a shoestring budget and traveled to the jungle to shoot the cover image of this book. That photo is 100% real and NOT Photoshoped.
**Attention James Cameron: She needs a job:** *ilo-wow@hotmail.com*

**Carmen Sipes** — *(Kaltxì Palulukan on title page and copyright page, ikran on copyright page)*
Carmen's creativity knows very few bounds. She is the artist extraordinaire who co-created such works as *Tony the Palulukan* (Tawtute Flakes), *Kaltxì Palulukan*, *Radio Avatar's* "World's first nerd Na'vi" logo, and several other *Avatar* movie cartoon characters that have brought much enjoyment to the fans of *Avatar*. If you have a paying gig you can reach her at *sipes.carmen@gmail.com*

**Mike Reitmeyer** — *("Looking for an Easy Way to Learn Na'vi?" image; top back cover)*
Mike Reitmeyer created the top main image on the back cover. He has graciously consented to allow us to showcase his art on the back cover book. He is available for commission work as his schedule allows.

He can be reached at *mikereitmeyer@gmail.com*

**Anatoliba** — *(Na'vigation cartoon; bottom back cover)*
The "Na'vigation cartoon was generously provided free of charge for use on the back cover of this book (bottom left). We hope you enjoyed it. The artist can be reached at *hensel.welzow@freenet.de* for professional inquiries.

KALTXÌ PALULUKAN!

**Dusty White** — *(the nut-job who dreamed up this arguably insane idea)*
*Avatar* came out on Dusty White's birthday and he immediately considered it a personal gift from James Cameron. Dusty conceived of and wrote *Learn Na'vi the Easy Way* in early 2009 and went on to create *Radio Avatar*, a fan-based podcast about "All Things Avatar." He originally created *Kaltxì Palulukan* as a spoof of Hello Kitty but with the generous help of Carmen Sipes was able to bring it to life. He is a *Learnnavi.org* moderator and the author and designer of this book.

Made in the USA
San Bernardino, CA
15 June 2016